Praise for
A Return to Self

"Ambitious in scope and impressive in its execution, this blended nonfiction work holds two truths at once: humanity's tendency toward destruction and discrimination, as well as its compulsion toward connection. Author and journalist Aatish Taseer succeeds in crafting a philosophically sound book with an approachable and enriching conclusion exploring the transformative power of empathy."

—Felicia Reich, a *Paste* Most Anticipated Book of the Year

"In *A Return to Self,* Aatish Taseer shows us how to see the world: He reveals what's beneath the facades, what we're missing, how it's all connected—and also how it all feels, tastes, and smells. He takes us deeper, while understanding that the surface is a reality too."

—Benjamin Moser, Pulitzer Prize–winning author of
Sontag: Her Life and Work

"Taseer's fascinating pilgrimage of identity and memory covers vast distances and centuries. Across continents, he makes unexpected connections between cultures and countries, histories and absences, belonging and exile. There is courage in what he says. The history of our world is personal."

—Darryl Pinckney, author of *Come Back in September*

"*A Return to Self* invites readers on a captivating expedition, painting vivid and intimate portraits in which every detail is a gem to be lingered on. As Taseer navigates the ancient cities of Samarkand, the lush greenery of Sri Lanka, and the historical marvels of Istanbul, he also embarks on an introspective journey, exploring the intersections of culture, memory, self-discovery, and what it means to belong."

—Clarissa Ward, author of *On All Fronts: The Education of a Journalist*

"From the high Andes to the heart of Mongolia, Aatish Taseer writes as captivatingly about history, spirituality, and the senses as he does poignantly. These essays, suffused with themes of connection and separation, deliver a lyrical meditation on how traveling far from home can bring you closer to yourself."

—Maya Jasanoff, author of *The Dawn Watch*

"At once restless and meditative, *A Return to Self* is a writer's journey into the liminal spaces—of memory, nationality, culture, and sexuality—that we inhabit. From a collection of moving and erudite travel pieces, Aatish Taseer brilliantly creates a portrait of the outsider, whose search for belonging defines the age in which we live."

—Tash Aw, author of *Strangers on a Pier*

"Writers I admire travel to discover other states of mind. But the even more admirable ones travel also to find new parts of their most authentic selves. In these pages, Taseer is such a traveler: the maps he is working with are those of the world, and also of the body, the soul, and the senses. His findings are fascinating and rich."   —Amitava Kumar, author of *My Beloved Life*

*A Return
to Self*

ALSO BY AATISH TASEER

A Return
to Self

EXCURSIONS IN EXILE

Aatish Taseer

CATAPULT
NEW YORK

A RETURN TO SELF

First Catapult edition: 2025

The essays in this book first appeared in *T: The New York Times Style Magazine* between 2019 and 2024.

ISBN: 978-1-64622-279-7

Library of Congress Control Number: 2024951088

Jacket design by Gregg Kulick
Jacket image © Maxime Corzet / Millennium Images, UK
Book design by Laura Berry

Catapult
New York, NY
books.catapult.co

Printed in the United States of America

1 3 5 7 9 10 8 6 4 2

For Ryan, who held me aloft when every
certainty around me crumbled

To awaken to history was to cease to live instinctively. It was to begin to see oneself and one's group the way the outside world saw one; and it was to know a kind of rage.

—V. S. NAIPAUL,
India: A Million Mutinies Now

But, ultimately, what today is the meaning of foreign, the meaning of homeland? . . . When the homeland becomes foreign, the foreign becomes the homeland.

—THOMAS MANN

CONTENTS

INTRODUCTION

The Demands of Belonging

ON NOVEMBER 7, 2019, THE GOVERNMENT OF PRIME Minister Narendra Modi revoked my Overseas Citizenship of India, or OCI, effectively banning me from the country I grew up in. India was where my mother and grandmother lived. Where four out of my five books of fiction and nonfiction were set. Where I had moved back after college in the United States with the aim of being "an Indian writer."

The pretext the government used was that I had concealed the Pakistani origins of my father. It was an odd accusation. I had written a book, *Stranger to History* (2009), and published many articles about my father, despite being estranged from him for most of my life. The story of our relationship was well known because my father, Salmaan Taseer, had been the governor of Punjab, Pakistan's most populous province, and was assassinated by his own bodyguard in 2011 for defending a Christian woman accused of blasphemy.

None of this had, until 2019, affected my status in India, where I had lived for thirty of my forty years. I became "Pakistani" in the eyes of Modi's government—and, more importantly, "Muslim," because religious identity in India is mostly patrilineal and more a matter of blood than faith—only after I wrote a cover story about Narendra Modi for *Time* titled "India's Divider in Chief." The article enraged the prime minister, who was in the midst of a reelection campaign. The headline, his louring image on the cover, framed within that famous red border, which in the Indian imagination had for so long been associated with prestige, sent Modi's supporters into a fury. In the days and weeks that followed, his troll army vandalized my Wikipedia page, accusing me of working as a "PR manager" for the opposition Congress Party; they began online petitions denouncing me; they ran amok on social media, making death threats, posting memes of me with a Pakistani eyepatch. *Time* magazine was inundated with hate mail at the rate of hundreds of letters an hour.

Then Modi himself said: "*Time* magazine is foreign. The writer has also said he comes from a Pakistani political family. That is enough for his credibility."

After that, my days in India were numbered. It did not matter that my mother was Indian. I had been recast as an outsider, an alien, a Pakistani. It was a judgment from which there was no reprieve.

In August, I received a letter from the Home Ministry threatening me with the cancellation of my OCI. Then, in November, an Indian news site leaked what the government was planning to do. Within hours, the Home Ministry's spokesperson was on Twitter, canceling my citizenship before I had been officially informed. In one stroke, Modi's government cut me off from the country I had written and thought about my whole life, and where all the people I had grown up with still lived.

TO LOSE ONE'S country is to know an intimate shame, like being disowned by a parent, turned out of one's home. Your country is so bound up with your sense of self that you do not realize what a ballast it has been until it is gone. It is one of the few things we are allowed to take for granted, and it is the basis of our curiosity about other places. Without a country we are adrift, like people whose inability to love another is linked to an inability to love themselves.

India was my country. The relationship was so instinctive that, like an unwritten constitution, I had never before felt it necessary to articulate it. I could say I was Indian because I had grown up there, because I knew its festivals and languages, and because my books were steeped in its concerns and anxieties. I was a British citizen by birth—the OCI was a substitute for dual citizenship—and, even though love had taken me to the United States, I returned to India frequently to write about it and visit the only family I had ever known. But to say as much was already to express a degree of removal that felt false. It was like making a case for why one's name was one's name. I was Indian because I just was. It was fundamental, a priori. Now that it had been questioned in this letter from the Home Ministry, I felt an odd sense of pity—*not* for myself, but for my family in India. I thought of my grand-mother who had raised me. I thought of how she had met the unconventionality of my mother's situation—an unmarried woman bearing the love child of a Pakistani—with unques-tioned love. That love had given me my sense of belonging. I thought of how outraged she would be to learn that those bonds of affection by which she had bound me to my place were being questioned—and by the prime minister, no less.

MY PARENTS MET in Delhi in 1980. My father had just writ-ten a biography of his political idol, Zulfikar Ali Bhutto; my mother was sent to interview him. That night they went to dinner at a Chinese restaurant called the House of Ming. Then they disappeared together for a week. Not long after my fa-ther left India, my mother discovered she was pregnant. There was no question of keeping the baby. The bad blood between India and Pakistan was not an abstract thing: my mother's Sikh family had lost everything during the 1947 Partition and came as refugees to Delhi. For my mother now to be pregnant by a citizen of that enemy country was unthinkable, not to mention that my father was married at the time, with three small children. In a week when my mother had gone to an abortion clinic with a girlfriend, my father called unexpect-edly from the Marbella Club in Dubai. She told him what happened, and by the end of their conversation, according to her telling, he had persuaded her to keep the baby—me. They had no plan beyond cobbling together a partially secret life, spent between London and Dubai. It lasted two years and ended badly. In 1982, my mother returned to India, where she reported on conflict—the secessionist movement in Punjab, the insurgency in Kashmir, civil war in Sri Lanka, the election and downfall of Benazir Bhutto. My father had returned to Pakistan to fight military dictatorship alongside Bhutto, suffering jail and torture. The last time they met was in 1990, during a general election that Bhutto lost, and wherein my father apparently tried to seduce my mother again.

The loss of my country was literal on one level—I could not go back to India—but also abstract: the loss of an idea, that "exalted" idea of a secular India. India, as its first prime minister, Jawaharlal Nehru, vowed, was not meant to be a "Hindu Pakistan." Rather, it was to be a place that cherished the array of religions, languages, ethnicities, and cultures that had taken root over fifty centuries. Nehru's idea of India as a palimpsest, where "layer upon layer of thought and reverie had been inscribed, and yet no succeeding layer has completely hidden or erased what has been written previously," served as the foundation for the modern republic, born of British colonial rule in 1947. The new country redefined secularism, away from the French idea of *laïcité*, to mean—as the parliamentarian Shashi Tharoor told me in 2019—"the existence of a profusion of religions, all of which were allowed and encouraged by the state to flourish." The idea of India was a historical recognition that over time—and not always peacefully—a great diversity had collected on the Indian subcontinent. The modern republic, as a reflection of that history, would belong not to any one group, but to all groups in equal measure.

As a young man, discovering Pakistan for the first time,

I had missed that Indian variety. The sudden imposition of homogeneity upon a composite culture was a shock. It affected values, and the assumption of homogeneity in my father's house—the jibes against Hindus, Jews, gays, Blacks, and Americans, the language untempered by the awareness of others—was more alien to me than anything else.

In India, I suppose I always knew that beneath the topsoil of the modern country, a mere seven decades old, there lay an older reality, embodied in the word *Bharat*, which evokes the idea of India as a holy land, belonging specifically to its 85 percent Hindu majority. *India* and *Bharat*—these two words for the same place represent a core tension within the nation. *Bharat* is Sanskrit, and the name by which India knows herself in her own languages, free of the gaze of outsiders. *India* is Latin, and its etymology alone—the Sanskrit *sindhu* for "river," turning into *hind* in Persian, and then into *indos* in Greek, meaning the Indus—reveals a long history of seeing oneself through Western eyes. India is a land; Bharat is a people—the Hindus. India is historical; Bharat is mythical. India is an overarching and inclusionary idea; Bharat is atavistic, emotional, exclusionary.

It was this tension between modern country and holy land—that the founder of Hindu nationalism, Vinayak Damodar Savarkar, took aim at in the early twentieth century. As he wrote in his 1923 book, *Hindutva: Who Is a Hindu?*, "To be a Hindu means a person who sees this land, from the Indus River to the sea, as his country but also as his Holy Land." This Hindu person was, in Savarkar's view, the paramount Indian citizen. Everyone else was at best a guest and at worst the bastard child of foreign invasion.

———

GROWING UP IN 1980s India, in a westernized enclave where, to quote Edward Said, the "main tenet was that everything of consequence either had happened or would happen in the West," I had no idea of this other wholeness called Bharat. That ignorance of Hindu ways and beliefs was not mine alone, but symptomatic of the English-speaking elite, which, in imitation of the British colonial classes, lived in isolation from the country around them. Mohandas Gandhi, at the 1916 opening of Banaras Hindu University, a project that was designed to bridge the distance between Hindu tradition and Western-style modernity, worried that India's "educated men" were becoming "foreigners in their own land," unable to speak to the "heart of the nation." Working closely with Nehru, Gandhi had been a great explainer, continually translating what came from outside into Indian idiom and tradition.

By the time I was an adult, the urban elites and the "heart of the nation" had lost the means to communicate. The elites lived in a state of gated comfort, oblivious to the hard realities of Indian life—poverty and unemployment, of course, but also urban ruin and environmental degradation. The schools their children attended set them at a great remove from India, on the levels of language, religion, and culture. Every feature of their life was designed, to quote Robert Byron on the English in India, to blunt their "natural interest in the country and sympathy with its people." Their life was, culturally speaking, an adjunct to Western Europe and America; their values were a hybrid, in which India was served nominally while the West was reduced to a source of permissiveness and materialism. They thought they lived in a world where the "idea of India" reigned supreme—but all the while, the constituency for this idea was being steadily eroded. It was Bharat that was ascendant. India's leaders today speak with contempt of the principles on which this young nation was founded. They look back instead to the timeless glories of the Hindu past. They scorn the "Khan Market gang"—a reference to a fashionable market near where I grew up that has become a metonym for the Indian elite. Hindu nationalists trace a direct line between the foreign occupiers who destroyed the Hindu past—first Muslims, then the British—and India's westernized elite (and India's Muslims), whom they see as heirs to foreign occupation, still enjoying the privileges of plunder.

Almost thirty years ago, in the preface to his book *Imaginary Homelands*, Salman Rushdie, fearful of the "religious militancy" threatening "the foundations of the secular state," had expressed alarm that "there is no commonly used Hindustani word for 'secularism'; the importance of the secular ideal in India has simply been assumed, in a rather unexamined way." As it happens, the exalted idea of India has no commonly used translation either. Rushdie was saying that this is not merely a failure of language, but an expression of the isolation of an elite that thought its power was inviolable. "And yet," Rushdie wrote, "if the secularist principle were abandoned, India could simply explode."

In 2014, I covered Modi's election out of the temple town of Varanasi, curled around the Ganges. I had grown up as a member of that English-speaking elite in India. I had lived among people who exercised a tremendous amount of economic and political power over a country they lived at a tremendous distance from. The precarity of their position had frightened me when I moved back to India after college in the United States. I felt I was living among people awaiting destruction. All my books dealt with how this class of person had made itself vulnerable in the new India. When Modi appeared on the horizon, I felt he represented a valid critique of the world he meant to supplant, without necessarily being the agent of a better one.

Here's an uncomfortable question: Did my own uncertainty about belonging in India—as the illegitimate son of a Pakistani, a gay man, a westernized product of a westernized elite—contribute to my need to make common cause with a Hindu majority whose passions I did not share?

My time in India as an adult was spent almost entirely trying to make up for the cultural and linguistic gaps of a colonial childhood. I learned Hindi and Urdu well enough to translate a major short story writer into English. I devoted hours every day to learning Sanskrit, the language of classical India. I traveled widely, trying to overcome the discomfort I felt in small-town and rural India. I eschewed sexuality as a basis for identity out of fear that it would leave me further isolated in my country. I killed off aspects of myself—my knowledge of French, my ease in the world beyond, not just in the West, but in places like Turkey, Syria, and Iran, where my first book was set—in order to better fit back into Indian life. I said earlier that one's relationship to one's country ought to be instinctive, effortless, something one might even take for granted. My relationship with India was anything but.

In the end, none of it mattered. In August, I received a letter warning me of the Home Ministry's intention to revoke my Overseas Citizenship of India. A few months later, in November—after the Ministry's spokeswoman canceled my OCI on Twitter, in response to a report in the Indian press—I walked over to the Indian consulate, on East 65th Street, and handed in the one document that had allowed me to live and work in India.

I was done. My mother, operating out of that old Indian sense of prestige and influence, had thought we might be able to finagle a tourist visa. Five years on, it is yet to materialize.

"Exile is a writer's natural state," the writer Jeet Thayil told the Indian press when asked about what the Indian government had done to me. It is a romantic idea, bringing to mind so many writers and painters, from James, Nabokov, and Joyce to Goya, Chagall, and Dalí, who were fed as artists by the experience—now imposed, now voluntary—of not being able to return home. But for each of these artists, there were countless more who lacked the inner resources needed to be away from their friends and family—not to say, their material—for so long. For them, exile is sterile. They lived away, and yearned for home, finding comfort in expatriate communities, slowly losing touch with their homeland, dying as artists.

I did not know which category I fell into, but as the reality of not being able to go home set in, an unexpected emotion crept over me. I felt relief. The burden of trying to fit into

India, of forever apologizing for its shortcomings, apologizing for my own Westernization, was suddenly lifted from me. The West, in turn, was no longer some dirty secret that I could enjoy only at the detriment of the "real" India. It was all I had. I was home.

The only analogous experience to the lightness I felt upon losing my country was borne in on me (no less strangely) soon after my father was killed. He had died a hero's death—like the old Thane of Cawdor in *Macbeth*, where, "Nothing in his life became him like the leaving it"—and he was mourned publicly by the likes of Hillary Clinton and Pope Benedict, who said a prayer for him in the Sistine Chapel. I felt the pressure to mourn him as others were mourning him, but, in my life, he had only ever been a heavy scolding presence. I feared his judgment, here related to my work, there to my sexuality, but now, upon his death, I felt the strain of having to see him as others saw him.

The writer V. S. Naipaul was my mentor and a friend in those days. We were at his house in Wiltshire soon after my father's assassination. He asked me how I was feeling. I began speaking of my father in a way that must have struck him as false, because he stopped me dead.

"But your father," he said, "was your great enemy, so you must also be relieved that he's dead." It was the kind of absolution only a writer can offer. I had tried so hard to be my father's son, suppressed whole sides of my personality, only to run into futility, that it was a relief to no longer have to try. He was gone, and I was free.

India was not an estranged parent, but the experience of

striving to belong in a place where one is destined to always feel a fraud was not dissimilar. My husband, whom I met in New York the summer of 2014, after the election that brought Modi to power, remembers how strenuous my assertions of belonging were at the time. The more I stressed my Indianness, the more he doubted it was real. I struck him as someone trying too hard. In the first years of our marriage, India was like a mistress. I would spend several weeks a year there, guilty about living away. But even at the best of times, India asserted belonging through a pact of mutual hardship. It was the opposite of America: it offered nothing, not opportunity, not comfort, not recognition. Endurance was the mark of true belonging. The perversity of these demands must have been hard on my husband. Not just my absences, but my need to forever balance two (if not three) societies in my head. I remember him asking me once to "unpack"—to not live as if my life in America were provisional.

Then suddenly one day I woke up to find it was the only life I had. Without it, I would have been on a one-way flight to Britain, where I had been born, but had no life to speak of. Once India closed behind me in the way that it did, the legal reality of not being able to go back merging with the hatred of Modi's supporters, I felt strangely free. I no longer had to make India seem better than it was (the bad air, the traffic), and the need no longer to lie—truth, in a word—felt like sustenance. So too did the return of my old curiosities. I could revel in my love of the English language without fearing that I was somehow letting down the side.

My first book had taken me to Turkey, Syria, and Iran.

I had thought nothing then, aged twenty-five, of renting an apartment in Damascus, or interviewing people in Tehran. The ability to do so was a direct result of my Indian upbringing. India knew centuries of Muslim rule, overlaid by two centuries of Britain colonization; India, in turn, fertilized the cultures of Asia as far east as Bali. All this was part of its natural cosmopolitanism. But, in the India I grew up in, and the India I returned to, none of this was of interest. India cared about India, and, in material terms, about the affluent West, which was ever a source of appeal and neurotic oversensitivity. The places in between, to which India had bonds of trade, language, history, and religion, mattered not at all in modern India. Living there, it felt like yet another side of myself I would have to shed in order to fit back in. At age twenty-five, due in no small part to my Indian background, my world had been multipolar. Back in India, it was an odious binary. I felt more in thrall to the West, living in India, than I ever did living in the West. India provincialized me.

I had begun to travel seriously again even before the Modi government seized my OCI. In February 2019, Hanya Yanagihara (my editor at *T Magazine*, for whom all these essays were written) sent me to Morocco to explore the vanished world of Saharan trade routes. In October that year, I went to Uzbekistan, traveling through the caravan cities of the old Silk Road. It was in these places of flux and continuity that I realized I was intensely concerned with what people perceived as theirs, what they saw as having come from outside—the demands of belonging, in a word. In Turkey, my first trip after Modi banned me from India, I confronted a former self, in the place where my life as a writer had begun twenty years before. It was a chance for me to see what I had gained and what I had lost in balancing my responsibility to myself against that of what one feels toward one's country. In Mexico, using the metaphor of food, I looked at how imaginary the idea of what is native, what invasive, truly is, despite the power it exerts over our loyalties. Similarly, within perfume there had always existed the category of the "orientals," related to strong smells such as musk and civet; but, at certain times in the history of European perfume, those smells had become the site of aversion and repugnance, as well as attraction and fantasy. Nothing about the way we imbue the world with ideas of belonging—what is ours, what is alien—is incidental. Tracing the legacy of Muslim Spain, I considered the ways in which integral aspects of a nation's history can, through the lens of religio-nationalism—in this case that of Le Reconquista—be reconfigured to seem nonnative, a contaminant. No doubt I was thinking of how Hindu India, which fell to Islamic armies within a year of Visigothic Spain—711 and 712—was turning away from its rich syncretic culture, questing after imagined notions of purity. In India and Sri Lanka, where I travel for the penultimate essay, the lotus is a religious symbol of purity, even as it has been co-opted by the ethno-nationalist parties of both countries. I follow the flower out of the nourishing mud in which it grows—*pankaja* in Sanskrit means "mud-born"—into the world of religion, art, and politics, exploring the illusion of purity, and the ways in which it is deployed.

The last of these essays and, by far, the longest, concerns pilgrimage. Three pilgrimages across three great faiths, *fiesta* in the high Andes, a spring of pilgrimage in Shaman and Buddhist Mongolia, culminating with Ashura in Iraq, the Shia mourning for the martyrdom of the Prophet Muhammad's grandson, Hussein, in 680. What interested me more than the spiritual aspects of pilgrimage was the way it created an idea of home in a distant land. I was intrigued by how the sacred could be both imperishable as well as liable to be reconsecrated. To me, pilgrimage was one of the great metaphors for the ties that bind and those we are prepared to shrug off. It replicated an atmosphere of exile, since it invariably took place in an unfamiliar setting, a place away from home, even as it brought nearer the indestructible idea of home and belonging that we each carry within us.

If these essays feel like a return to self, it is because they represent the return of my natural curiosities and, dare I say it, cosmopolitanism, after the long night of cutting away parts of myself in order to better fit back into Indian life. They are a response to the illusion of the idea of home. The strand of elation that runs through them is the simple joy of being out in the world, free of the pressures of belonging. Perhaps there could not have been any other response, given that my country, my material, my world in India, had been snatched from me. I grew up in what felt to me like the crucible of all anxieties related to belonging. Those anxieties run through these essays, but they are also a tribute to the individual. After all the wringing of wrists, the stewing over questions of place, of feeling myself forever betwixt and between, I woke up one day to find the bars of my prison had magically disappeared, and, far from being scared, I felt a new vein of intellectual curiosity had opened for me. With the idea of home gone, I stepped out into the world again.

A Return to Self

Istanbul

AT 9:05 A.M. ON THE TENTH OF NOVEMBER, 2020, A hush fell over the leaden turbulence of the Bosporus. All activity on the strait ceased. Coast Guard ships, ferries, and caïques, like the younger members of a tribe of large marine mammals, drew close in a circle. Behind them, a Turkish destroyer kept vigil, the blue of its gunmetal merging with the strait's frigid waters. A red-bottomed freighter marked with the words IRAQI LINE hulked in the background. That cityscape of sea-blackened buildings, broad panes glazed silver in the daytime darkness, was no ordinary Left Bank, no mere farther shore. The silhouette of low domes and pencil-thin minarets piercing a nimbus of pale sky above was the continent of Asia. The wonder of looking at it, with my feet still planted on the shores of Europe, was not lost on me. I had been in Istanbul for less than seventy-two hours. The air grew heavy with anticipation, and then, low and deep and melancholy as whale song, came the first moan of a ship's horn.

Everyone froze. The uniformed figure of an old sea captain snapped to salute. A stout woman in a long black coat with a blue headscarf drew her toddler near. Even the seagulls, whose cawing and mewling were so much a part of the commotion of the Bosporus, fell in line with this solemn tableau. The air was soon resounding with ship horns and sirens. The moment of remembrance stretched out. Its object, Mustafa Kemal Atatürk, founder of the Turkish Republic, stared out at me from the backs of two young Turks, where his youthful likeness was emblazoned on the red ground of the Turkish flags the pair wore as superhero capes around their necks. The Father of Turks, blue-eyed and visionary, with a touch of the derring-do of the old Omar Sharif about him, had died eighty-two years ago at exactly 9:05 a.m. in Dolmabahçe Palace behind me—an overcooked nineteenth-century confection of pilasters and sleeping columns. We stood on its manicured grounds, speckled with magnolia and spruce, remembering the fierce secularist who in the 1920s had fought off European incursions on all sides and founded a modern republic from the wreckage of the Ottoman Empire.

I was engaged in a remembrance of my own. As 9:06 rolled around and people stirred again, I awoke to the fact that I had seen all this before. I had traveled not only through space, but through time, journeying to a place where a younger self was waiting for me. Fifteen years earlier, I had stood at the edge of this very same waterway, witnessing this very same scene. Practically all my adult life lay between the last time

I had come to this city, as an aspiring writer of twenty-five, ready to travel through the Muslim world for a book I had yet to write—from Istanbul to Mecca, and from Mecca to Lahore—and now, when, a few weeks away from forty, I had returned to Istanbul. Why? Was it to look again at what had become of the world I had traveled through in 2005? Was it to look again at what had become of me? What I knew, walking back through plane-lined boulevards draped with Turkish flags, Atatürk's speeches blaring out of rows of freestanding speakers on the pavement, was what I felt: paralysis.

"YOU CAN GO back many times to the same place," says a character in V. S. Naipaul's 1979 novel, *A Bend in the River*, "and something strange happens if you go back often enough. You stop grieving for the past. You see that the past is something in your mind alone, that it doesn't exist in real life. You trample on the past, you crush it. In the beginning it is like trampling on a garden. In the end you are just walking on ground."

Istanbul was not flat ground for me. It was still very much a garden, the perfectly preserved repository of the hopes, ambitions, and confusions of my twenty-five-year-old self. That first morning, I was so nervous about disturbing the overlay of memory that I entertained fantasies of not venturing out into the city at all. I imagined spending whole days in the sanitized security of my room at the Swissôtel, where I had paid $45 extra per night for a view of the Bosporus, gazing out at the sun-lit splendor of the most beautiful body of water in the world.

I would live on room service, swim fifty lengths a day in the hotel's indoor pool, and return a week later to New York City with my memories of Istanbul intact. My anxiety was akin to what one feels after a big snow when one fears nothing so much as the sight of those first tracks on its surface, knowing they will ensure the destruction of what until that moment had been pristine.

The city I had returned to was bathed in rare November sunshine. The Bosporus, which, by way of the Dardanelles, connects the Black Sea with the empyrean blue of the Aegean, with what the travel writer Jan Morris has called "waters of Homeric myth and yearning," was in a bright, inviting mood. I used to think it was the geography of Istanbul that was special, that extraordinary location of old Byzantium—the Greek colony that would form the nucleus of the future city—peering out at the confluence of three waterways: the Bosporus, the Sea of Marmara, and the estuary that is the Golden Horn. Antiquity had regarded those who built their city on the eastern side of the strait—the poor inhabitants of Chalcedon, the town on the facing shore—as blind for failing to see the superiority of the site for Byzantium. Now, of course, it was all Istanbul, a seething megalopolis of 15 million set over hills of dark, furrowed pine.

As far as I know, only three cities through history—Rome, Istanbul, and New York—have been referred to as "the city." The word *Istanbul* itself is a contraction of the Greek phrase *eis ten polin*: "into the city." One imagines it as the superior reply to a question from someone in the outer boroughs. "Where are you going?" "I'm going into the city, of course!"

Grand as it was, even this city of cities paled before the glory of the Bosporus. As the sixteenth-century French topographer Pierre Gilles observed, the Bosporus "is the first creator of Byzantium, greater and more important than Byzas," the founder of Byzantium. There is nothing on earth quite like it. Imagine the splendor of the Grand Canal in Venice married to the international shipping glamour of the Suez or Panama Canals. Over forty thousand vessels pass through the strait annually, about two and three times the traffic, respectively, of Suez and Panama. But the true singularity of the Bosporus lies on its shores, where the grand, seemingly incompatible binaries of Islam and Christendom, Asia and Europe, East and West, stand opposite each other, at times only half a mile apart. The strait itself remains as neutral as the sky, ever-changing, ever-unreliable, like some people-pleasing friend aware of the pressures of having to be everything to everyone.

On my first morning, it was decidedly Greek. With the sun exposing deep veins of aquamarine and boats of every size tracing foamy zigzags over its surface, it seemed to flow inexorably south. To look at Istanbul then was to feel myself on the edge of a maritime culture of fresh fish and shrub-covered islands, where goats with metal bells pick their way around whitewashed churches. The hulking mass of the Hagia Sophia, the sixth-century church that became the enduring symbol of Christendom, seemed like a basilica to me again, surrounded by a copse of slim, tapered minarets. But scarcely two days later, the clouds were racing and the water had darkened. Now the Bosporus seemed to flow north to that cold lakelike sea of villages of blackened wood, sloping muddy streets, and red-bearded men with bright blue eyes. All of a sudden, Istanbul had become a Balkan city of lowering skies.

The Bosporus dramatized dualities. It did not resolve them. Here, one lived in a perpetual state of cultural whiplash. The perturbation one felt in Istanbul came from having to carry the city's myriad selves in mind at once. Protean city! It could change on a dime, and one had to be ready to change with it, as the city itself had so many times through history—from Constantine's New Rome of AD 330 to the premier city of Islam after its capture by the Ottomans in 1453—or be left nursing a sense of betrayal.

THE JAGGED, UNRESOLVED character of Istanbul fit the mood of my arrival in 2005. I was living then with what felt like irreconcilable differences within me: I was Indian but three years before had met my Pakistani father for the first time, a man whose absence had overwhelmed my younger years. I was gay but dating a woman. I was living in London but was on my way home to India, by land, via Syria, Iran, and Pakistan. I wanted to be a writer but had just quit my job as a reporter at *Time* magazine. The journey I was to make, which was a reckoning with my father's absence—but also with Islam and the legacy of India and Pakistan's 1947 Partition—was part of that original need for wholeness, of imagining I could write myself free of the gaps in my life.

I can say all this now in easy declarative sentences, but it has taken me half a lifetime to work through the tangled mass in which these competing identities existed in me at the age of twenty-five. Then, I was full of rage. I was drinking a lot. I was ready to reckon with one side of myself, the political and historical, but I was running from another: the sexual. "A man whose desire is to be something separate from himself . . . invariably succeeds in being what he wants to be," writes Oscar Wilde in *De Profundis* (1905). "That is his punishment. Those who want a mask have to wear it."

I certainly was wearing a mask when I arrived then, but I did not want to be separate from myself. The eight months of travel that lay ahead, in stripping away the edifice of habit, into which all enduring lies insinuate themselves, would bring me to a truer self. But only after much pain—mine, of course, but also that of those around me.

At the time, my girlfriend and I were at the beginning of an extraordinary journey. We had dropped south from Venice through the ghost lands of the old Ottoman Empire. My girlfriend was of a grand family; her parents were minor English royals. In Bulgaria, at a hunting lodge outside Sofia called Vrana, we stayed with her cousin. He was a tall, elegant figure in his late sixties, and he had been both the king and the prime minister of Bulgaria. Arriving late by overnight train from Budapest, he greeted us at the door of his palace, which was all dark wood and deep eaves. It had been taken over by the Communists for half a century, he explained, but when he returned to it in 1996 after the fall of Communism, he found it exactly as he had left it as a child. "They stole the silver," he joked, but every other piece of furniture, which had been put into a vault, was meticulously restored. Sitting under a Klimt light, eating lamb chops that he had prepared, we listened to stories of the great figures of the twentieth century: Wallis Simpson and Edward VIII, the shah of Iran and Lillibet, his name for the queen. In my notebook I wrote: "One of the funniest stories he told us the other night was of Lillibet welcoming the president of Portugal after Salazar. They were watching a display of the queen's horses and a couple of them farted loudly. After this happened several times, Lillibet whispered to the Portuguese president, 'I'm sorry.' To this, the president of Portugal replied, 'Oh, I thought it was the horse!'"

It was exciting to travel like this. There was an air of the innocence of prewar Europe about the journey. It reminded me of the opening stanza of T. S. Eliot's "The Waste Land" (1922): "And when we were children, staying at the archduke's, / My cousin's, he took me out on a sled, / And I was frightened." In Istanbul, thanks again to my girlfriend's connections, we were put up in a hotel, owned by one of Turkey's richest families, on Taksim Square.

I am standing in that square now. I am with Eyüp Özer. In 2005, this young Marxist student, whom I had met by chance at a book launch, had acted as my guide and translator. This is the first time we have set eyes on each other since I left Istanbul fifteen years ago. Eyüp, too, is almost forty now, with much less hair, the lines of his rugged features more deeply etched. Still a Marxist, he works for a metalworkers' union. Through Eyüp, I had seen firsthand the rising wave of Islamism sweeping Turkey. In 2005, Prime Minister Recep Tayyip Erdoğan had been recently elected and seemed like the bright new hope of liberal Islamist democracy. He had aspirations of Turkey joining the European Union. But fifteen years on, dealing in a combustible mixture of historical nostalgia and nationalism that had swept the world from New Delhi to Washington, Erdoğan had turned nakedly authoritarian. Under him, Turkey consistently set global records for jailing journalists. "Our country has become much more conservative," Eyüp said, "but young people are much more skeptical."

Eyüp and I had had almost no contact all these years, and as we walked through an Istanbul of gentrifying neighborhoods, now all cafes, vintage shops, wine bars, and design studios, where there had once been crumbling oriel windows and weed-encrusted corbels, we tried to close the gap between past and present, alternating between the political and the personal, occasionally touching on those rare events that were a mixture of both. Eyüp had read of my father's assassination in 2011. My father belonged to a westernized elite in Lahore that was very similar to the Turkish Kemalist elite—the avowedly secular followers of Atatürk, at whose remembrance I had only just been—whose members, for the most part, ruled Turkey for eighty of its hundred-odd years as a modern republic. In 2009, just a few months before my book about my father was published, he became the governor of the Pakistani province of Punjab. In office, he had sought clemency for a poor Christian woman accused of blasphemy. This action alone released a firestorm of religious anger against him. Then, on a dismal winter day in January 2011, he was gunned down by his own bodyguard. His killer became a religious hero in Pakistan and my book was used, writes the journalist Declan Walsh in *The Nine Lives of Pakistan* (2020), "to portray Taseer as a fallen

Muslim," adding that "in Islamabad, devotees still flocked to the glittering tomb where Taseer's assassin lay buried."

Eyüp and I spoke of Pakistan, aware that a similar revolution, of class garbed in faith, had taken place in Turkey, too. He reminded me about the religious students we had spoken to at an Islamic cultural center on the Asian side. "We have a platonic love for the state," they had said. "We love the state, but it doesn't love us back."

"Now," Eyüp added with a bitter chuckle, "they have the state."

Turkey's secularism had been extreme. Headscarves were banned in public buildings; the state selected the country's clergy, or ulema, and closely monitored their sermons for the slightest expression of religiosity; prayer beads or facial hair were viewed with suspicion. Many whom we spoke to then had seen Turkish secularism as the means by which an entitled Kemalist oligarchy preserved its power.

On Taksim Square, now cut through with tunnels and underpasses, Eyüp pointed out the scene of a violent confrontation in 2013 between Erdoğan's regime and its critics, many of whom were university students. Every inch of this city had been fought over. In Gezi Park, protests against its development were put down with brute force and, three years later, in 2016, when sections of Turkey's military, traditionally the protector of its secular state culture, attempted a coup against the regime and failed, Erdoğan was handed the perfect opportunity to purge every aspect of public life, from the army to academia, of his political opponents.

Even as we spoke of politics, Eyüp and I were circling

around changes nearer to home. At a coffee shop on İstiklal, a major pedestrian thoroughfare, which had lost its wonderful air of political foment and beer-drinking students in side alleys—it now possessed a McDonald's, a Starbucks, and a Sunglass Hut—Eyüp said, "Personal things have changed a lot, too. You never stay as you are when you're twenty-three."

Here was an opening to confront the elephant that had accompanied us on our walk through Istanbul. In 2005, I had a girlfriend. Today, as Eyüp likely knew from my Instagram, I was married to a tall white man from Tennessee. I needed to catch Eyüp up on that cataclysm in my personal life, but I had a built-in reluctance to speak of my sexuality outside the safety of cities like New York. I was habitually discreet about it when traveling, but my hesitations around Eyüp had more to do with what a mess I had been, sexually speaking, the last time I saw him at age twenty-five. Sex with men, even then, had always been part of my life, forming an unbroken arc from preadolescence into adulthood. But at that age, I lacked the means to connect desire with love, and I had never been in a relationship with anyone who identified as gay.

In Istanbul, when I had last encountered Eyüp, I had found a gay life that was much closer to what I had grown up with in India. Though still deeply closeted, on that visit I was a regular at the Firuzağa hammam, set among the winding cobblestone streets of the Çukurcuma neighborhood. It was nice to come in from the cold, stash one's clothes in a locker, and wander through the squalid warren of marble-floored rooms, the domes pierced with tiny oculi, which allowed in a frosted, ethereal light. In the main room, scalloped with marble basins, there was a semblance of decorum, but in the side rooms, the men were young and frisky. We touched each other freely under our *peshtemal*, the small Turkish towels we were given. If things got too hot, we peeled off in twos and threes to more private alcoves. I remember a lot of laughter and playfulness, and then I remember walking back to Taksim Square, through the dark, winding streets, afraid of disease, afraid the wet hair around my ears would give me away to my girlfriend. I was at once deeply gratified and wretched with guilt.

The call to prayer sounded, jolting me out of this memory. Eyüp sat in front of me, framed against a background of flower sellers and ATMs, a mnemonic in the flesh. I wanted to use this moment to unite the person I had been then with the person I was now. Biting the bullet, I said, "I'm married to a man now."

"I know," he said. "And that's great."

It was done. I felt instantly lighter. I saw my past self, surrendering his claim on the real estate of memory, allowing me to unite divided realities.

My younger self had been uneasy with the gay rights movement as I watched it play out in the West. For a long time, I rationalized it to myself, feeling that we in the East had more urgent questions to deal with than sexuality. I told myself that we in places like India were in the grip of great human convulsions surrounding questions of history, religion, and politics. Sexuality felt like the kind of fine-tuning that only rich Western societies could indulge in once the bigger issues had been put to rest. India, which would soon find itself in the throes of a majoritarian religious populism akin to Turkey's, felt unsafe for so many groups of people— liberals, women, lower castes, its Muslim minority of about 200 million—that perhaps I believed, in 2005, that freedom functioned like a queue, and sexual orientation came last, some final frontier that only people in near-perfect societies could afford to deal with.

As Eyüp and I walked on, the Bosporus appearing down cambered streets in corridors of molten platinum, I thought of the tendency we in countries like India and Turkey had of putting grand abstractions before concrete ideas of personal freedom and happiness. At the Hagia Sophia, the call to prayer was sounding for the first time in some eighty-five years. In July of 2020, Erdoğan had turned what had been a basilica for over nine hundred years, a mosque for almost five hundred, and a museum in the modern era back into a mosque. The change embodied the mixture of historical nostalgia and abstract passion that energized his authoritarian rule. Watching the throng outside washing for prayer in the golden sunshine, I asked Eyüp if people supported the Hagia Sophia's reversion to a mosque. The answer he gave me stood as a perfect encapsulation of what I had been telling him earlier, of the fervor the demagogue provides when he cannot provide a daily wage and a good job. "Before, even hard-line Islamists did not care about it," Eyüp said, "but once Erdoğan raised it, everybody loved it and they jumped on the bandwagon."

We stopped short at the entrance. A green-and-gold mosaic of the Madonna with child looked down on a constant stream of devotees in headscarves and heavily veiled women in black. "That's a strange choice of entrance for a mosque," Eyüp said with a grin. He didn't want to go in. The pandemic was raging in the city. Numbers were spiking, but because the Turkish lira was in free fall, the authorities were resisting the economic hardship of another lockdown.

THIS RETURN TO Istanbul, bridging the chasm of years, felt like a return to self. But in more concrete ways, the theme of exile was all around me, too. On the Galata Bridge, with its permanent fixture of anglers, rods hovering over the silver water of the Golden Horn like so many tiny tower cranes, Eyüp, glimpsing the traffic of Uzbeks, Syrians, Afghans, and Africans, said, "It has become a refugee city."

Of the close to 3.8 million Syrians in Turkey, at least 540,000 lived in Istanbul. "There is huge racism against them," Eyüp said. After my time in Turkey in 2005, I had taken the overnight train from Istanbul to Aleppo and spent almost three months in Syria's capital of Damascus. I was haunted by the fate of that country.

It was why I now sought out Ibrahim M., a thirty-year-old from the northwestern Syrian city of Idlib. He had been arrested twice, first by the Assad regime, which imprisoned and tortured him, and then by the Islamists who had taken over his region of the now-Balkanized country. Ibrahim had come to Istanbul via the southern Turkish province of Hatay, and he was one of at least hundreds of thousands who now lived in a partial state of limbo in Turkey. He came to me through a Syrian acquaintance living in New York, who had been part of the volunteer organization known as the Syria Civil Defense, or the White Helmets.

He met me at my hotel. He was dressed in close-fitting jeans, wore aviators, and appeared muscular under his thick maroon sweater. The reddish tint of his beard, his hazel eyes, and pale skin gave him the air of someone from the Black Sea or the Caucasus. In the taxi over to one of the many Syrian enclaves that had appeared in Istanbul, Ibrahim was quick to tell me that, though he could barely afford it, he lived with his wife and six-year-old daughter in Galata, where people were kinder to foreigners. "I cannot say that people are racist," he said, choosing his words carefully, "but I cannot say they are not." When I asked him a political question about Syria, he froze, indicating that we should not speak of these things in the taxi. He later explained that while he had some basic papers that allowed him to be in Istanbul, his wife had none. His application for Turkish citizenship (which was eventually granted in September 2021) had been held up owing to security concerns. His parents had gotten theirs, but they were in Hatay. Ibrahim had not seen them in three years.

The neighborhood of Fatih, with its beautiful fifteenth-century Ottoman mosque of low domes and pointed minarets sheathed in bluish lead, and its delicate linden and plane trees, had turned into a little Syria. Eyüp and I had spent a fair amount of time here in 2005, but it was unrecognizable now. Ibrahim led me through street after street abounding with Syrian sweet shops, supermarkets, perfumeries, and restaurants. At Buuzecedi, a famous Damascene restaurant, men in bomber jackets sat at small, close-set tables, hunched over tea and falafel. "It's just like Damascus inside," Ibrahim said. We stopped at supermarkets packed with cheese and dates and fava beans, which were used to cook *foul*, a cumin-seasoned stew. Ibrahim had me taste freshly made pastries such as *knafeh* and *hulwa*, which the baker pressed into a bed of fragranced pistachio before handing it to me. Ibrahim said he came to this neighborhood once a month to get all his rations.

His nerves had abated while we were in the Syrian enclave, but as we wandered down a sloping street that culminated in a ministry for foreigners and immigrants with a long line outside, his fears returned. "It was full of harsh," he said of his fifty-four days in Assad's prison, where he had been sent for participating in the demonstrations that followed the Arab Spring. "These are not my real teeth. I lost my hair. I lost my mind."

Ibrahim could not afford to take Turkey for granted. It was all he had. Outside the ministry, he had seen two men in uniforms whom he referred to as "the red police." They were vigilantes, known locally as "Erdoğan's sons," who could haul him in at any time and question him. They could separate him from his wife and their daughter. In that moment, I felt all the precariousness of his life in Turkey, the closeness of the trauma in Syria, and the uncertainty of being practically stateless. Like a man reflecting on the spent passion of youth, he said, "I must stay and remain quiet."

Ibrahim spoke more directly to me than he might have imagined. I could no more return to India than he could return to Syria. I had been living with the dull pain of exile these many months but hadn't realized, until that moment, how much my need to meet someone like Ibrahim and my grief over what had happened in Syria were a sublimated version of my own for India. What we thought was home no longer existed.

"If one loses [one's own country]," writes the German journalist Sebastian Haffner in his memoir, *Defying Hitler* (1939), as translated by Oliver Pretzel, "one almost loses the right to love any other country." Without that delightful game of give-and-take, of receiving and offering hospitality, of discovering new places out of the security of having one's own, Haffner continues, one becomes "a man without a shadow, without a background, at best tolerated somewhere."

Ibrahim and I stood that afternoon on a precipice overlooking a city of terra-cotta roofs. Behind us, the domes of the sixteenth-century Süleymaniye Mosque, the masterpiece of the greatest of all Ottoman architects, Sinan, loomed. Ahead, under wheeling flights of gulls, cloud shadows had appeared on the Bosporus, inky blots that gave an illusion of stillness, even as they raced over the quicksilver face of the strait. Ibrahim, who was determined to turn his back on Syria and look only to the future, said he wanted eventually, as his brother already had, to go to Europe. "But I don't want to go in the illegal way," he said. "I can't risk my daughter."

AS MY TIME in Istanbul drew to an end, my past in the city lost its special edge. I was able to restore truer ways of feeling to certain memories that a younger, more fearful self had falsified and that the passage of time had made inviolate.

In 2005, I had left this city in a fever dream of bottled-up desire. A gay couple I had been staying with after my girl-friend went back to England for Christmas had taken me on my last night to a club called Love. There, in a dark room bathed in black light, man-smelling, stale with sweat and co-logne, a show was about to begin. On a stage were four men in white briefs, their shaved bodies taut and sinewy. They held great globs of neon green and orange paint in their hands. The music began. A hush fell over the crowd. In the purple shade, the men danced closer together, their thighs brushing against one another's. The first green gash of paint across the torso of one of the men sent the crowd into a frenzy. The paint changed hands, the tempo rose, the men pawed each other freely, using touch and color to shake off their invisibility.

Arousal gave way to fulfillment. Beautiful young Turkish men paired off. I felt devastated about the lie that stopped me from joining them. I wrote about that night in my book, giving it a political cast, but not about how I had truly felt. Life is full of unanswered desires, but there is a special regret about those weaknesses that prevent us from being more fully ourselves. The next morning, as snow began to fall over Istan-bul, I boarded the Taurus Express for Aleppo, brimming with unconfessed yearning.

"I can't compete with the other intimacies in your life," my girlfriend told me the following year, 2006, once we were back in London. Love and sex by then had ceased to be dis-connected for me, and I was deep in the middle of an intense but toxic love affair with a young man who also had a girl-friend and who was also ostensibly straight. It was a horrible, painful quadrangle in which deceit fed passion, and it was a relief to be released from it. But I was to spend many more years in India in a state of sexual limbo, trying desperately to compartmentalize my desire for men, before I could come to a true place of transparency, a place where the inner and outer lives were one.

"Look, men have been sleeping with men for thousands of years," James Baldwin tells Richard Goldstein in "Go the Way Your Blood Beats," a 1984 interview for *The Village Voice*, "and raising tribes. This is a Western sickness, it really is. It's an artificial division. Men will be sleeping with each other when the trumpet sounds. It's only this infantile culture which has made such a big deal of it." At twenty-five, though I disliked secrecy, nothing seemed more natural to me than dating women and occasionally having sex with men.

I thought about Baldwin a lot on this second trip to Istanbul. From 1961, for about ten years on and off, this city had been a refuge to him. Quoting Baldwin's biographer Fern Marja Eckman, Magdalena J. Zaborowska writes in *James Baldwin's Turkish Decade: Erotics of Exile* (2009), "whenever closer hideaways fail to immunize him against his own social susceptibility," he came to Istanbul, adding that the city served him "as a neither-here-nor-there liminal space."

If Baldwin had shown me why I was justified in feeling as I had about sexual identity at the age of twenty-five, he also showed me how I was wrong. For one, societies do not deal comprehensively with a single area of human freedom— be it gender, race, or religion—before moving on to another. As Baldwin himself saw, "The sexual question and the racial question have always been intertwined," and a society must fight for justice on many fronts at once. Two—and more important—I owed my entire happiness to the gay rights movement that had made it possible for me to live in safety with my husband in New York.

Looking out now on the mirrored face of Istanbul, this city of sky and water with its many moods, I was happy to have exchanged grander narratives for feeling easier in my skin. Sexuality was not everything, but nor was it so imperfect a barometer of our quest to be more truly ourselves. It was good to return to New York, having acted on what Baldwin had felt was not so much advice as a mere observation: "If you don't live the only life you have, you won't live some other life, you won't live any life at all."

A Journey of the Senses

Perfume

1. A Childhood in India

I REMEMBER AS IF IT WERE YESTERDAY THAT DISTANT afternoon on which I first smelled *oudh*. I was in my grandmother's house in Delhi. I was thirteen, maybe fourteen. We had a family perfumer, or *attarwallah*, a man of some refinement, who came to us from Lucknow—a city that serves as shorthand for high Indo-Islamic culture. We didn't know the attarwallah's name, or how he knew to follow us from address to change of address. But he came without fail two or three times a year. A slim, gliding figure, with a mouth reddened from *paan*, or betel leaf and areca nut, the attarwallah produced his wares from carved bottles of colored glass that he carried in a black leather doctor's bag. He showed us scents according to which season we were in. So in winter, musk and patchouli; in summer, white-flowered varieties of jasmine—of which there are some forty-odd in India—as well as rose and vetiver. In the monsoon, he brought us *mitti attar*, which imitates the smell of parched earth exhaling after the first rain (*mitti* means "mud" in Hindi). The perfumes came from the medieval Indian town of Kannauj, which is a seventy-five-mile drive west of Lucknow and which, like its French counterpart, Grasse, has a tradition of perfume manufacturing several centuries old. Once he had drawn his perfume out on white cotton buds at the tips of long, thin sticks, the attarwallah lingered over his customers, telling stories of the various scents and reciting the odd romantic couplet of Urdu poetry.

It was this attarwallah's son who came one day to see us, bearing news of his father's passing—and of oudh. It was immediately apparent that the attarwallah's son was a man apart from his father. He had kohled eyes and wore drab beige trousers, and where his father had been full of Old World charm, the young attarwallah was oily, pushy, and a tiny bit sleazy. Once the women of the house—my mother, my grandmother, my aunts—had commiserated with him over his father, they took an instant aversion to him.

It was winter. Orange-barred heaters glowed in the room where the attarwallah and the women sat. I was listening to them talk of quality and seasonability when the young perfumer, with all the indelicacy of a greenhorn, announced, "I have some oudh."

A hush fell over the room.

"How much?" my mother whispered, as if the young perfumer had tried to sell her hashish and not perfume.

"What's oudh?" I said, no doubt in response to the magical effect this word had had on the room. The young attarwallah, perhaps relieved to see a friendly face in this tough crowd, was upon me like a sprite. I was drinking masala tea and, before I could say another word, he let fall a single drop of oudh into the cup.

"Drink it now," he said with a smile.

I took a sip and—my God!—my senses were scrambled. I was engulfed by a synesthesia as pure and overwhelming as any Baudelaire ever knew. It smelled—or did it taste?—like a deep, woody mustiness, a kind of fragranced shade, the tantalizing cool of a covered bazaar. It was familiar, almost banal, like the scent of sacks of grain and spice in an old godown, but also somehow glamorous—sensual, velvety. It was heavy, enchantingly in lockstep with the smoky winter day outside, but not lugubrious. It drew me nearer—to smell a little was to want to smell more—but it never fully gave up its secret. It produced an illusion of comfort, like that of an old *shahtoosh* shawl, but it was arousing, too, stirring memories of places I had never been, sensations I had never known. No sooner had that first layer peeled away than I sought to possess it, like a man in a fever dream clutching at the air.

Part of what I was feeling had to do with the nature of smell itself. Of the senses, smell alone has a direct line to our limbic system, the part of our mind that deals with emotions and memory. The urgency we feel in the midst of a profound odor-related experience, of memory rushing ahead of words and reason, can be physiologically explained: the olfactory nerve sends signals directly to the emotion-memory part of our brain without going through the relay junction of the dorsal thalamus the way the other senses do.

I came out of my reverie to see an inert drop of oil colliding aimlessly against the porcelain edge of my teacup. I was hooked. I wanted some oudh, and I wanted it then and there. My mother shook her head. A vial of oudh, even in the early 1990s, in an India creeping out of socialism, cost several hundred dollars.

Of course, the reason it was so expensive only made me want it more. Oudh is an oleoresin, born out of a fungal attack upon the heartwood of a perfectly ordinary slim-limbed tree, native to South and Southeast Asia, known as *Aquilaria malaccensis*. Undiseased, the tree is a mere evergreen. But once the fungus has struck, gradually transforming the weight of the tree so that it can no longer float in water—"the Chinese name for the material is *ch'en hsiang*, 'sinking fragrance,' the Japanese *jinko*," wrote Edwin T. Morris in 1984's *Fragrance: The Story of Perfume from Cleopatra to Chanel*—the precious ooze, elixir of sickness and decay, appears, turning the woody innards of the tree to liquid gold. The fungus strikes only certain trees, and one must wait up to half a century for the highest-quality yield. That is why oudh is so expensive, and why many years would go by before, thanks to the generosity of a family friend, I would acquire a few meager ounces of the precious resin—some oudh of one's own.

To grow up in India in the wake of colonization, as a child of the 1980s, was to learn to balance multiple societies in one's mind, without ever quite achieving resolution or overlap. "When you have a double culture," Francis Kurkdjian, fifty-two, a French perfumer with Armenian roots and the creator behind such evocative scents as Jean Paul Gaultier's Le Male (1995), said to me recently, "you are more open, because as a child you experience something on the side, which allows you to have another window on the world."

In terms of fragrance, what this meant for me was that I occupied two worlds that remained separate, unassimilable. There was traditional India, the world of the attarwallah, with all its smells: of the moist matting screens of vetiver in old houses in the summer; of cool sandalwood paste, or *chandan*, in the temple, smeared on one's forehead after a ritual; or of the smoking brass vessel of frankincense, or *luban*, carried through the house in the evenings to purify the air. What I could not have known, as an "oriental" boy growing up among oriental smells, was that, from the late 1970s through the mid-1980s, a movement was underway in Western perfumery, in which the scents of my childhood, known in fragrance as the "orientals"—ambers and aromatic woods, vetiver, patchouli, musk, and sandalwood—were being repurposed. Their rise, culminating eventually in the popularization of oudh in our century, spoke of profound societal changes in the West, such as women's liberation, sexual freedom, and the global dominance of the United States.

Of these new strong scents that represented the arrival of the independent woman, not unlike my own mother—who was among the first female journalists in India to cover conflicts—none perhaps was as distinctive as one belonging to a particular bottle that sat on her dressing table. It had a strange burnt-orange casing, shaped (I now know) like an *inro*, one of the small Japanese boxes, with tiny compartments containing medicinal herbs, seals, spices, and opium, that the samurai wore on their belts. On the curvilinear face of the bottle, like that of a hip flask, was a glass oculus through which a rich, amber-colored liquid was visible. Dull gold letters on the front read OPIUM PARFUM YVES SAINT LAURENT. I remember its heavy, intoxicating odor, all spice, patchouli, and balsam. In its baroque suggestion of luxury, it was of a piece with the gold-bordered silk brocade saris my mother wore out on winter evenings in Delhi.

In 1978, the year after Opium was first released, Edward Said published his seminal work, *Orientalism*, which posited the idea of a newly rapacious West, arising out of colonialism, taking ownership of Eastern culture and history as a means to have authority over it, to speak for it and, as a consequence, to better control it. "Indeed, my real argument," Said wrote, "is that Orientalism is—and does not simply represent—a considerable dimension of modern political-intellectual culture, and as such has less to do with the Orient than it does with 'our' world." Said's study concerned itself mostly with art, literature, and history, but what was true of other aspects of culture was true of perfume, too: The rise of the orientals in the late 1970s, of which Opium was emblematic, marked one of many moments when the West was speaking through the East of things that had more to do with the West than with the East. There is something fascinating to me (though rarely benign) in the idea of another, more powerful culture, expressing itself through yours—cultivating, as Said writes, "one of its deepest and most recurring images of the Other."

In this way, the rise of the so-called orientals is not merely a story of a particular vogue within perfumery; it is the story of seduction, power, history, and legacy. Above all, it is inextricably tied to the birth of modernity in Europe.

2. The Arrival of Crude Intensity

A DECADE IN perfume, as in art, is never just a calendar decade. The 1980s heralded an era of bold, sensual perfumes, which decisively began a few years earlier with the arrival of Opium. This decade of license and promiscuity came abruptly to an end in the mid-1980s as the full horror of the AIDS epidemic became apparent. "People realized," the perfumer Kilian Hennessy, forty-nine, said, "that sex can kill." Sex and death became inextricably and tragically linked, and the effect on perfume—which makes as much material use of decay as it does the fresh buds of spring, and thus has a deep connection to the cycle of creation and disintegration—was profound.

"Perfume is very sociological," Hennessy continued. "It is always an emanation, a reflection, a mirror of the society." Hennessy, who is arch and self-assured, and has the studied seriousness of someone who also has a naughtier side, is a marvelous perfumer, who I believe is the inspiration for the nose, or perfumer, on Netflix's *Emily in Paris*. ("No comment," he said when I asked him, though he will not deny it outright.) To him, the 1980s was defined by shoulder pads, pantsuits, and ambitious women—such as Sigourney Weaver in *Working Girl* (1988)—who needed, he feels, "strong perfumes so that they could feel strong in a masculine environment."

"We gave them Opium from Yves Saint Laurent," he said, making me wonder whom he meant by "we." "We gave them Coco from Chanel [1984]. We gave them Poison from Dior [1985]." To this list, Hennessy added Charlie by Revlon (1973), Oscar by Oscar de la Renta (1977), and Obsession by Calvin Klein (1985), saying, "If people ask you, 'What were the 1980s?' it smelled like Poison in France and it smelled like Obsession in America." The latter fragrance, in a smooth-contoured bottle, was a blend of pure musk and animality, primal as the fossilized DNA of our species preserved in amber. The former was so strong that there were signs in Michelin-starred restaurants in France banning women wearing the Dior fragrance. And that was Hennessy's point: this was an era in which crude intensity stood in for real strength.

Chantal Roos, who was responsible for marketing Opium in the 1970s, agreed with this assessment. Roos rose to the heights of French cosmetics at a time when it was not easy for women to do so. "When we arrived with Opium," Roos said over FaceTime from her apartment in Paris, "it was a hit, but it was a scandal." Financially, the fragrance was a runaway success. "It was immediately attractive to women of all generations," Roos said. "Very oriental, very sensual, very sexy." Young girls lined up at shops to pay for it in advance.

Today, of course, a brand could never market a perfume like Opium the way Roos did. As much as Opium spoke of sexual freedom, women's empowerment and a new American boldness, it had nothing at all to say to the culture of China, in which it had dressed itself. It was, if anything, actively offensive. The People's Republic of China banned the fragrance.

In the United States, Chinese Americans protested the scent, objecting to the commodification of a narcotic that had caused China so much pain in the nineteenth century when, during the Opium Wars, Britain turned the powerful nation into one of addicts. "Opium," Roos said, speaking somewhat nostalgically of the past of a country that was not hers, "was the dream of the empress of China."

But while Yves Saint Laurent may have fetishized the East, making it say what he wanted it to say, he was working in what was already a rich tradition in France, going back at least as far as the nineteenth-century orientalist paintings of Jean-Léon Gérôme and Horace Vernet and the exploits of Gustave Flaubert's *Voyage en Orient* (1849–51). "We may as well recognize," writes Said, in describing why Europe needed this idea of the "licentious" East, "that for nineteenth-century Europe, with its increasing *embourgeoisement*, sex had been institutionalized to a very considerable degree. On the one hand, there was no such thing as 'free' sex, and on the other, sex in society entailed a web of legal, moral, even political and economic obligations of a detailed and certainly encumbering sort." The more constrained the West felt, the more it turned the East into "a place where one could look for sexual experience unobtainable in Europe."

The harm in making another society the theater of one's forbidden desires, however, is that one ends up robbing that place of agency. Flaubert created the stereotype of an "oriental woman" as sensual, submissive, the object of white male desire and dominance. In gesturing to the appeal of such a figure for Flaubert, Said stresses the loss of a right to speak: "What he especially liked about her was that she seemed to place no demands on him, while the 'nauseating odor' of her bedbugs mingled enchantingly with the 'scent of her skin, which was dripping with sandalwood.'" To be clear, this is not the sacred chandan that was smeared on my forehead during Hindu ritual. This is something altogether more profane. And Said makes an important point: "There is very little consent to be found, for example, in the fact that Flaubert's encounter with an Egyptian courtesan produced a widely influential model of the Oriental woman; she never spoke of herself, she never represented her emotions, presence, or history. *He* spoke for and represented her."

At the same time, contra Said, one should be careful not to overstate the power of the West over the East. The East, after all, continues to have an autonomous relationship with its own scents. No one smelling sandalwood in the sanctum sanctorum of a temple in Varanasi is thinking of Flaubert's "oriental woman"; nor, when the laundry comes back in the summer smelling of vetiver, does one self-orientalize, as it were. Just as the relationship of the women in my house to the attarwallah was direct, free of the West as a conduit, so, too, do any number of people living in India, Saudi Arabia, and other parts of Asia engage with their own smells on their own terms, according to their own seasons and traditions, free of the Western gaze.

I'm not even entirely sure animality, with all its associations to sexuality, is a Western imposition. Consider the Sanskrit court poet Kalidasa, in whose verses we encounter a river scented with the fragrant ichor of wild elephants. In *The Birth of Kumara*, Kalidasa's fourth- and fifth-century masterpiece (translated by David Smith in 2005), which dramatizes the love of Shiva, the great god, destroyer of worlds, and Parvati, a goddess of fertility and divine strength, Shiva wanders among cedar hills "sprayed by Gangetic cascades, whose waters are scented with musk from the navel of the musk deer." In the last canto, an epic romp called Consummation, Shiva drinks in Parvati's sweat-covered body, and they make love all night, leaving the "coverlet creased and uneven, streaked with red dye from their feet." Here, still centuries away from the colonial gaze, one snatch of verse returns hauntingly, providing what may be the last word on sex, smell, and perfumery: "What is pure and what is dirty?"

3. A Rose Is a Rose Is a Rose

YET HOW DID florals figure in this history? For early modern Europe, as in India today, perfume had many functions, from medical to religious, that went well beyond its use as an expression of an individual's taste, personality, and toilette. But toward the end of the eighteenth century and the beginning of the nineteenth, a change began to occur in European society that would forever alter the position of floral scents—violet, orange blossom, tuberose, acacia, jasmine, and rose—in relation to their heavier oriental counterparts. To understand the privileged position florals would acquire in the nineteenth century, as well as their association with purity, cleanliness, and femininity (or what the historian Alain Corbin describes in *The Foul and the Fragrant: Odor and the French Social*

Imagination [1982] as the "mysterious collusion between woman and flower"), one needs to recognize how intimately the change was connected to the collapse of premodern society itself. The rise of Corbin's "deodorized bourgeoisie" in nineteenth-century Europe, along with the discovery of pneumatic chemistry, which discounted the therapeutic role of healing vapors (recall the plague doctor with his beaklike mask full of aromatics) led to a new world where the only good smell was no smell; or, at best, a light floral. "Among the elite," writes Corbin, "changes in tastes and in fashion sanctioned the experts' discrediting of heavy scents. The smells of private space became less strong and were enriched and varied by more delicate and subtle fragrances." In a Europe emerging from the bubonic plague, from cramped cities prone to pestilence and fire, there was an increased "fascination with airy space." The London of 1665 in Daniel Defoe's *A Journal of the Plague Year* (1722) is full of vapors, distempers, and deadly odors. Defoe describes people as walking in the middle of the street, so as not to "mingle with anybody that came out of the houses, or meet with smells and scent from houses that might be infected." These streets of mud, in which the dead were laid out, also swarmed with "a wicked generation of pretenders to magic, to the black art, as they called it."

It is this premodern past that Europe by the nineteenth century was turning its back on. In this new world, florals became representative of public sanitation; the division between public and private; the rise of the individual, science, and reason; and the loss of God, to whom—through incense, heavy woods, and resins conveyed through a veil of blue smoke and mystery—our earliest notions of perfume itself are tied. In the new world, now free of liturgy and magic, "the balsamic effluvia of springtime meadows," writes Corbin, "became an obsession." In Giovanni Battista Tiepolo's paintings, with their emphasis on interiors, Corbin sees the "expression of a new sensitivity to smell," of wanting to shut out the odoriferous world beyond.

The rise of the "orientals" in the late 1970s, of which Opium was symbolic, marked one of many moments when the West was speaking through the East. To me, witnessing a similar change in the India of today—from the stress on individuality to the rise of smaller families in enclosed, apartment-like settings, representing a movement away from tradition to modernity, from rural to urban—is like being granted a view of what nineteenth-century Europe must have felt like, a new society where "personal toilette as an aspect of good manners" was "being codified in an increasingly strict and precise manner," as Corbin writes. It was the scent of florals that became the breath of this new, disease-free Europe. As had happened so often in the past, the notion of physical cleanliness became synonymous with moral hygiene. Light fragrances were associated with chastity and purity, while heavier smells—balsams, musk, amber, heavy woods, and leather—were banished to the brothel.

"When you put too much perfume on," said Kurkdjian, making explicit the connection between strong perfume and depravity, "you smell like a cocotte. A whore, basically. Intense perfume for the nineteenth century was linked to having a bad life." That attitude prevailed well into the twentieth century, so much so that when Coco Chanel was on the eve of launching her Chanel No. 5 (1921), "she wanted a perfume," writes Tilar J. Mazzeo in *The Secret of Chanel No. 5* (2010), "that would be sexy and provocative and utterly clean." The fragrance—which, owing to its unparalleled success, is known in the industry simply as *le monstre*—was notable for its use of astringently fresh-smelling aldehydes that met the pared-down needs of twentieth-century modernity. (Was it coincidence that Ernest Beaux, the French nose behind No. 5, was born in Russia in the 1880s, part of the same generation as the poet Vladimir Mayakovsky and the painter Kazimir Malevich, who were remaking literature and art from the ground up?) "To Coco Chanel," Mazzeo adds, "the scent of overpowering musk, with its hints of unwashed bodies, was simply dirty. She understood immediately that it was the odor of prostitution, and it was unbearable."

4. The Fragrance of Sex

EVERY TIME A sea change of this kind between florals and orientals occurs, we have a tendency to believe that our tastes, our fashions, our palates, and, indeed, our morality are completely new, unprecedented, or final. In fact, the ebb and flow of florals and orientals is part of a dialectic over four hundred years old. Orientals were once celebrated for harnessing a kind of raw, sensuous animality.

Kurkdjian told me the story of how, in the sixteenth century, Henry IV of France had written to his mistress Gabrielle d'Estrées, instructing her, perhaps apocryphally, not to bathe when he came back from war because the smell of her un-bathed body was arousing. ("It's totally insane when you think about it now," Kurkdjian added.) Whether it was Madame du Barry, the official mistress of Louis XV, who was rumored to have been dripping in ambergris, or the Empress Joséphine, who was described as "*la folle du musc*" (mad for musk), the animalics of that century spoke of the body, naked, unwashed—the locus of all our desires. At times the raw power of that smell produced arousal, at other times revulsion. "I obeyed respectfully," writes Casanova in the eighteenth century of the elderly Duchess of Rufe, who demanded the seducer come sit next to her, "but a noxious smell of musk, which seemed to me almost corpselike, nearly upset me." As Corbin writes, paraphrasing the English essayist and physician Havelock Ellis (1859–1939), "Women did not use perfume to mask their odor but to emphasize it. Musk had the same function as corsets that accentuated the contours of the body."

"From a perfumer's point of view, the fresher perfumes are all about being clean," said Frédéric Malle, fifty-eight, the founder of Editions de Parfums Frédéric Malle; his grandfather cofounded Christian Dior Perfumes in 1947, and his mother later became the head of product design there. "When you wear an eau de cologne, it's an extension of your grooming routine. And you're saying, 'I'm clean.' The deeper you go, the darker you go, the closer you are to the skin, the closer you are to animality, the closer you are, by wearing one of these perfumes, whether you're wearing an evening dress or something very formal, you're shouting to the room, 'This is how I smell naked!' You don't even have to open your mouth."

The "animality" Malle spoke of was historically derived from three principal sources: ambergris, which came from a secretion in the intestines of the sperm whale that it used to coat the sharp beaks of cephalopods, such as squid and cuttle-fish, to make them digestible; civet, the glandular secretion of the titular cat, found in Africa and Asia, and which produced, Morris writes, "a revoltingly fecal odor" that "becomes both extremely agreeable and strongly fixative when blended with other essences"; and musk—the word *mushka* in Sanskrit literally means "scrotum"—which comes from a sac on the abdomen of the male musk deer, an animal predominant in Siberia and the Himalayas. It is significant that these scents did, for the most part, actually come from the Orient, as did pepper and silk. Yet the history of our associations does not match up exactly to the history of commerce. At any given moment, depending on our own sense of cultural confidence, we can, as societies, both enlarge or diminish the origin of a particular commodity. Sex and smell. It feels basic, it feels pri-mal. Who hasn't left a dirty weekend wearing the unwashed T-shirt of the person they've been shacked up with? Who hasn't known the role the evil, enticing smell of armpits can play in making the more painful aspects of sex—bottoming, for example—more bearable? Who hasn't reveled in the loop-ing playback of sexual imagery brought on by still being able to smell or taste someone on your lips? The perfumer on *Emily in Paris* adds indole, an aromatic compound, to the base notes "for some depth and richness," to his new olfactory creation, describing it as possessing the same molecular shape as *merde*. And as Rodrigo Flores-Roux, a perfumer at Givaudan, a Swiss fragrance and cosmetics company, observed, that same molecule, which is indeed present in the smell of fecal matter, is also present in mother's milk. "So you're talking about decay and new life at the same time," he has said about indoles. "I always use them, even in very, very small amounts, because it's important to remind us about the cycle of life and death."

5. In Search of a New Smell Abroad

IT WAS OUDH that gave me my first taste of the richness of Eastern perfumery, and not too long ago, in Malle's shop on Manhattan's Madison Avenue, I found myself reliving that childhood experience through an oudh fragrance—it's called Dawn, and one hundred milliliters costs $1,600—that the nose Carlos Benaïm, responsible for perfumes such as Polo Ralph Lauren, had recently created for Malle. Growing up in Tangier, where his father was a pharmacist, Benaïm said, "I was not aware that oudh existed." Not because it was hard to find but because it was ubiquitous. "It smells like oudh all over the place," he added. "The markets smell like that. And that is part of your construction." Here, again—and I think that is why he said it—we see a direct relationship between a perfumer like Benaïm, raised in the Islamic world, and a fragrance like oudh. Far from any connotation of sexuality, or even exoticism, it suggests a daily smell, the smell of the marketplace, which is exalted through the genius of perfume into something rare and special. It speaks of wealth and success, of course (oudh remains something an affluent Saudi man might give his wife as a present), but it has deep organic roots and,

like all true luxury, it takes what is familiar, almost banal—
the smell of dry earth after the first rain, say—and elevates it
to a cherished and coveted object.

The rise of oudh in the West, for Mathilde Laurent, Cart-
ier's in-house perfumer, was "associated with the fact that we
are living in a society where there's much more freedom as far
as gender is concerned," she said. Speaking to me from Paris,
Laurent, with platinum blond hair and a sideways-knotted
neck scarf, was the picture of aquiline French elegance. "I
think we went in search of a new smell abroad," she said, "a
smell that, because it comes from the Orient, doesn't have
a gender." The East, Laurent felt—and she was right—did
not have this "insane attitude" toward gendering perfume.
In India and parts of the Middle East, men wore rose and
women wore oudh (though it should be said that this gen-
derless approach to scent did not translate into societies that
were any less gendered). Laurent felt that this "reconquest of
orientality" was an example of the West listening better to
the East and not merely using it as an instrument to speak
for itself. Money made people listen, too. By the 1990s, Gulf
Arabs, now traveling more and more, were becoming a force
at the perfume counters of Harrods, Selfridges, and Bergdorf
Goodman. "You realize," Benaïm said, "that if you put an
oudh perfume in Harrods, it will sell at crazy prices. Everyone started to develop their own oudh line." For that reason,
oudh's success in the West is something apart from the orientalism of the 1980s. Here we see, after centuries of one region
co-opting another's right to speak for itself, cultural power beginning to flow the other way, East to West. But throughout

this olfactory journey, in which a new world of sensibility and history had opened up to me, one question remained paramount in my mind: What would perfume's response to the pandemic be, especially as COVID-19 menaced our ability to experience smell itself?

Boarding an Air France flight at the beginning of the year, Hennessy entered into business class, as successful perfumers do, and noticed a large bottle of Clarins Eau Dynamisante in the bathroom cabin. Cologne is essentially a disinfectant, containing 96 to 98 percent alcohol. Bathing himself in Eau Dynamisante, and taking unusual satisfaction in its antiseptic quality, the perfumer was returned to childhood memories of his mother rubbing him down with cologne to shield him from a threatening, germ-filled world beyond. His need to feel physically protected sent Hennessy back to a project that he had shelved months earlier. It was finalized the day we spoke.

"My next scent will be a cologne," Hennessy said. "And really, without the COVID, I probably would not have launched a cologne in my brand." Reaching into the history of his art, where, as the dictionary says, "the action of perfuming" is linked, at the root, to that of fumigation, Hennessy said, "Historically, colognes were a way to protect against the miasma." Then, pausing, perhaps afraid that I had not understood, he clarified: "Disease."

The Museum Cities

Uzbekistan

IT WAS OCTOBER IN TASHKENT. THE BROAD SOVIET-style avenues of Uzbekistan's capital were lined with chestnut and Oriental plane, their leaves turning russet in the crisp autumn air. This city of 2.5 million had, in Soviet days, which lasted from the 1920s until the country's independence in 1991, been the premier capital of Central Asia. It is home to more than half of Uzbekistan's 116 universities, and on that first golden morning in Tashkent, there was something of the glazed perfection of a Soviet propaganda poster in the sight of students in twos and threes strolling down the runway-size avenues. They were dwarfed by the giant buildings that lined the roads—banks, museums, and ministries—"Babylonian blocks," as the English writer Philip Glazebrook, who had been in Tashkent at the end of Soviet rule, described them in *Journey to Khiva* in the early 1990s: "Since the days of Nineveh this has been the architecture of dictatorship and persecution." And so it was, but after my late arrival on the Turkish Airlines flight from Istanbul, I found myself oddly in sympathy with the ideal, if not the reality, of Soviet life.

Four great creeds—Zoroastrianism, Buddhism, Islam, and Communism—had come via the trans-Asian caravan routes, or the Silk Road, to the land encapsulated by what is modern Uzbekistan.

Each had made the people of this doubly landlocked country—one of only two, the other being Liechtenstein—of 34 million part of a greater world, a cosmopolis, a comity of nations. This was a land whose culture had been created on the frontier of contact with China, India, Iran, and Russia, each of which fertilized the culture of the steppe. Communism was the last ideology to come to Uzbekistan along these routes, and I could not help but admire the scale and ambition of its artifacts. There was the Tashkent metro, twenty-two miles long, with majestic stations—several hung with three-tiered chandeliers—including one tiled in futuristic blue faience, dedicated exclusively to space exploration. There were the vast apartment blocks, with cramped windows and lace curtains.

Their facades were crawling with satellite dishes, and on their broad flanks, there were crumbling murals and mosaics, which had been made as if out of a desultory spirit of concession to the need for people to have ornamentation in their lives at all.

For me, as someone who grew up in Delhi, the names of this region's fabled caravan towns—Samarkand and Bukhara—were the most evocative of the Silk Road. Each estimated to be founded no later than the first century AD, these cities were imbued with the terror and wonder of the

Turkic conqueror Timur—known as Tamerlane in the West—who came like a fury over the mountains that lay between India and Uzbekistan and laid waste to my hometown in 1398, killing, by his own count, one hundred thousand and erecting his famous minaret of skulls. Some 120 years after Timur, his descendant Babur—a banished prince of the Timurid dynasty—came back over those same mountains to found the Mughal dynasty in North India, which lasted until the nineteenth century and was responsible for such marvels as the Taj Mahal. Delhi and Tashkent were just a three-hour flight apart from each other, but the girdle of mountains—the Hindu Kush, literally "Hindu Killer" in Persian—that separated this land from the Indian plain was a boundary between worlds. To arrive here was to find myself in the uncanniest of all valleys—a place where shared references to food, language, and architecture revealed the alien and unexpected.

My guide, Aziz, thirty-two, appeared magically out of the gloom of a cold and smoky night, dressed, like the hero in a Bollywood film, in a black-and-white gingham shirt, a Panama hat, and a scarf around his neck. Aziz was born in the twilight years of the Soviet Union and, as he pointed out to me, was among the last generation to grow up reading Soviet textbooks. Hearing him address a Vietnamese woman in Russian or seeing him point out Kazakhs, Koreans, Ukrainians, and Russians on Hazrati Imam—a square of mosques and madrassas at the heart of old Tashkent—I was reminded that Russia, no less than France or Britain or Spain, had been a colonial enterprise, and her subjects were myriad. But before I could take in my new surroundings that first morning, Aziz sprung a surprise on me. Ten months before, his longtime girlfriend, Madina, had left him and gone away to Dubai. He had suffered excruciating heartbreak, he told me. He couldn't sleep, he couldn't eat, he begged her to return. He then cast a sidelong glance at a shy young woman, sulky and watchful, with pink nails, who now also appeared out of the murk to join him. Madina was back. She had arrived unexpectedly the day before Aziz and I were to embark on a weeklong trip through Uzbekistan, covering a distance of over a thousand miles in close quarters.

Moreover, Aziz informed me, she was coming with us. Had the hour not been 3:00 a.m., had I not been so shattered from the twenty-hour odyssey from my home in New York City, and had I not been totally at Aziz's mercy in this foreign country, I would never have agreed to be the third wheel on my own trip. But the odds were not in my favor. Aziz, I sensed, was restless enough to cancel if I did not comply. I rolled a cigarette, nodded my consent, and from thereon vanished into the set of a modern-day Uzbek romance—Aziz and Madina, a love story.

THE TERM *SILK ROAD*, or *Seidenstrasse*, is thought to have been first popularized in 1877 by the German geographer Ferdinand Paul Wilhelm, Baron von Richthofen. It is misleading in many ways, not merely because much more than silk was conveyed along this four-thousand-mile ancient route—there was also lapis, turquoise, gold, and ivory—but because it was richer still in the traffic of abstractions, ideas, and religions. It came about a century before Christ, as a result of the mercantile interests of two great empires—imperial Rome and imperial

China—gradually aligning, even as they were too far apart to trade directly with one another. As a natural consequence, the places that lay between the two shouldered the responsibility (and accrued the profits) of bringing them into contact with each other. "Chinese merchants were never seen in Rome," writes the British historian Peter Hopkirk in 1980 in *Foreign Devils on the Silk Road*, "nor Roman traders in Ch'ang-an," referring to present-day Xi'an. It was in the time of the Han dynasty's Emperor Wudi (156–87 BC) that a great pioneering traveler named Zhang Qian, whom Hopkirk describes as "the father of the Silk Road," forged a path westward into modern-day Uzbekistan. Zhang went west in search of allies, in order to fight an enemy of nomadic stock—the Xiongnu—who some believe were the very same people who arrived a few centuries later at the gates of Rome (by then they would have been known as the Huns). In the Fergana Valley, which sprawls across eastern Uzbekistan, southern Kyrgyzstan, and northern Tajikistan, Zhang found something better than an ally—he found Ferghana horses, an essential machine of war in his emperor's fight against the Huns.

Meanwhile, imperial Rome, stretching its fingers east, had encountered a "revolutionary new material." In 53 BC, at Carrhae, seven Roman legions led by Marcus Licinius Crassus stared in disbelief as their habitual and, in this instance, victorious enemy, the Parthians, from modern-day Iran, "unfurled great banners" of a shimmering, gossamer-like material: Chinese silk. "The Romans, who had never seen anything like it before," Hopkirk tells us, "turned and fled, leaving some twenty thousand dead behind." The Romans knew that while the Parthians were a martial people, they were too "unsophisticated" to have invented "this astonishing material, which was 'as light as a cloud' and 'translucent as ice.'" By the first century AD, Romans were dripping in silk, which they still believed grew on trees. "Seneca, for one," writes Peter Frankopan in his 2015 history *The Silk Roads*, about the Roman philosopher, "was horrified by the popularity of the thin flowing material, declaring that silk garments could barely be called clothing given they hid neither the curves nor the decency of the ladies of Rome." The foundations of marriage itself were being compromised, Frankopan adds, by this fabric that "left little to the imagination."

The Silk Road is our supreme metaphor for the interplay between commodities and ideas—and, as an extension, the interplay between the intangible and the concrete. On my first day in Tashkent, I encountered an object that remade my idea of the history of the place. I had not, until then, thought of Tashkent as a great Islamic capital—not like Istanbul, Cairo, or Baghdad, say—but in the small Muyi Mubarak Library at Hazrati Imam, at the heart of old Tashkent, surrounded by ribbed azure domes swimming up against a pale sky, I saw what had to be among the wonders of the Islamic world: the oldest Quran in existence (best estimates date it to the eighth century). There it was, its swollen pages of gazelle skin inscribed with the bold black letters of the Kufic script. It had been the private Quran of the third caliph, Uthman ibn Affan, and it was Timur—the "scourge of God" in Christopher Marlowe's play *Tamburlaine the Great*—who, having laid siege to the civilized world in the fourteenth century, brought it from what is now Iraq to his capital at Samarkand. Its presence in Tashkent was a reminder that if one was to do justice to the history of Uzbekistan, one would have to make a mental separation between the modern state—an unremarkable Central Asian republic with an autocrat at its helm—and the many worlds this land had been part of. The state was new, the land was eons old. It had once comprised Sogdiana and parts of Transoxania; it had been a point of confluence between Iran and Turan, the line between Persianate and Turkic cultures; the famous regions of Khorasan and Khwarazm were all part of what the land had known. It had produced a roll call of polymaths, from the scholar and scientist al-Biruni to Ibn Sina, known to the West as Avicenna (980–1037), one of the fathers of early medicine. The creator of the algorithm—al-Khwarizmi (circa 780–circa 850)—had been part of the same flowering of genius that had made this land one of the centers of thought and discovery, as had the philosopher Alpharabius, or al-Farabi (circa 878–circa 950). This was the kingdom of the astronomer-king Ulugh Beg, whose fifteenth-century work was being translated into English and Latin in the years following the Renaissance.

This land of many natures—Turkic and Persian, upon which Russian had been grafted—expressed itself in Aziz, too. He was a Bukhara boy to his bones, raised in, and still devoted to, his birthplace. It was his passion for the history of his hometown that had connected him with other cities in Central Asia, forming the nucleus of a self-education, here from other guides, there from books in Farsi, English, and Russian. This was not so much a melting pot as a hologram, and this felt true of religious values, too: this was an Islamic country where everyone drank vodka and where the Soviet government, in the Communist years, had closed some twenty-six thousand mosques; there were just eighty open in 1989. But Islam had had its revenge. In a bookshop on the main square, Aziz pointed to a pamphlet that showed pictures of Lenin's statue being torn down as it warned against idolatry.

Aziz himself had undergone something of a Damascene unconversion. Madina remembered him as being very religious, praying five times a day and talking endlessly about the Quran. "But then," Aziz said, "I turned on my logic." He was now positively scornful of religious people, arguing with them about contentious subjects such as why, if Islam was a religion of peace, had it gone everywhere "by sword and fire."

"I am shocked," Madina said.

"It's a new life, baby," Aziz answered jauntily. He could not fathom Madina's restlessness, her wish to get away.

On our first full evening together in Tashkent, a still older and deeper aspect of the character of this land asserted itself as the sun sank—the nomadic life of the steppe. Chorsu Bazaar was in central Tashkent, a short drive away from Hazrati Imam. It was a vast carapace of turquoise and cyan, which sought to bring order to the chaos of one of the main institutions of Central Asian life: the market. Handsome Tajik boys with thick unibrows—a mark of beauty in the Persianate world—sold turmeric, cumin, red chile, and star anise. There was horsemeat and tongue, trotters and brain. We passed smooth, dark offerings of liver, reddish-black in the fluorescent light, and the round marbled heads of bovine cannons. There were whole alleys devoted to salads and cheeses, and sour-milk balls called *qurut*, which I was told quenched thirst on long journeys across the steppe. Outside, women with gold teeth in bright aprons and waistcoats sold *norin*, noodles with horsemeat. One plump-fingered lady cut me off a bit of *khasib*, a sausage made of rice and intestine, basting in a thick viscous liquid like a wounded snake. Chorsu, literally meaning "four streams" or "crossroads" in Persian, was visceral in the most literal sense of the word, and I felt it was impossible to come into contact with food like this without also being given an intimation of the brutality and rigors of the steppe. To never settle was to never be softened by the idea of home. It was easy to see how the decision to stay and build community, with all its implications for civilization, versus the decision to forge on and live the life of the frontier, was among the earliest and most important choices that men had had to make.

THE NEXT MORNING, we crossed the Jaxartes—also known as the Syr Darya, one of two great Central Asian rivers—and sped on through pale sunshine, yellowing screens of poplar and mulberry, and a pointillist field of cotton, a scorched brown crop bedaubed white, on our way to Samarkand. Aziz and Madina were asleep in the back seat. Our driver, Doniyor, a man in his fifties, spoke only one word of English—"good"— which he sometimes used as an exclamation and other times as a question. We passed vineyards and orchards. Melon season was ending and the pomegranates were ripening; women sold the dark juice in plastic bottles on the side of the highway. There were Tolstoyan scenes of soldiers picking cotton. I had expected desert and steppe. Instead, I found a dark, fertile soil, as rich as Andalusia, where everything from apples to apricots grew. Babur, the first Mughal, had been homesick in India for the sweetness of the fruits of his native land. In the beginning sections of his early sixteenth-century memoirs, *Baburnama*, there are endless descriptions of the fruit markets of Central Asia. I now began to see why. Autumn here was truly, as John Keats wrote, a "season of mists and mellow fruitfulness."

Before the galloping Russian conquest of the nineteenth century—the Russian Empire for over four centuries expanded at a rate of roughly twenty thousand square miles a year—the land of this country had been divided into two khanates: Kokand in the east and Khiva in the west. Sandwiched in the middle, and famous for cruelty, decay, and isolation, was the emirate of Bukhara, which included Samarkand. By the end of the nineteenth century, the khans and emirs had been reduced to puppet rulers, pensioners of the czar in Moscow. While the Silk Road, which increasingly became less relevant by the first quarter of the twentieth century, fed them with trinkets from an industrializing Europe—here a mechanical calendar, there a clock and a camera—a new creed was ascendant in Europe. In 1917, the Bolsheviks smashed the power of the czar. Two years later, the Communists, under the leadership of Mikhail Vasilyevich Frunze, were at the doors of these vassal kingdoms, driving their khans and emirs into exile.

It is hard to exaggerate the violence of the social and economic upheaval that Soviet rule brought to this country. The Uzbeks witnessed massive collectivization and industrialization; religion was proscribed; in 1927, Hujum, which means "assault" in Uzbek, was enacted under Stalin. These were social reforms that saw women give up the veil, participate in veil-burning ceremonies, and join the workforce.

Driving into Samarkand, 191 miles southwest from Tashkent, observing giant Timurid pylons and ribbed turquoise domes rising out of the low sprawl, I saw the change this society had seen in the last century inscribed in stone. Timur had breathed fire into the veins of the old Silk Road. He was born when the memory of the destruction that Genghis Khan had wrought was still fresh, and Timur, as if assimilating the fury of the great Mongol, had weaponized the ancient trade linkages. The map of his campaigns looks like an explosion out of Samarkand in every direction through the civilized world. He lashed out in the direction of Istanbul, taking the Ottoman sultan Bayezid I captive at the Battle of Ankara, south to Delhi, and died on the warpath east to China. It was not quite violence for violence's sake. "There was another equally, if not more, compelling reason to pick a fight," writes Justin Marozzi in *Tamerlane: Sword of Islam, Conqueror of the World*, his humanizing 2004 history of the tyrant. "Khorezm straddled the caravan routes linking China to the Mediterranean, and therefore enjoyed great prosperity." Timur turned the Silk Road into his personal exchequer, using its revenues, as well as plunder and taxes levied on conquered people, to fund campaign after terrifying campaign.

"If you doubt our power," Aziz said as we stood at the foot of Timur's statue in Samarkand, "look upon our buildings." It was the Timurid creed, and the evidence of its gigantomania was everywhere in this city. "In the one field in which he took a real interest," writes S. Frederick Starr in 2013, in *Lost Enlightenment*, of Timur, "and on which he showered money—architecture—his enthusiasm stemmed precisely from its ability to dramatize a very specific idea: that of his own power and greatness." The statue of this conqueror sat in the middle of a roundabout, surrounded by broad avenues, lined with the pale mottled trunks of Oriental planes. The man whose name was still uttered with horror and disgust in India gazed loftily upon his own mausoleum, Gur-e-Amir, a building that had been intended as a tomb for Timur's beloved grandson but became the Timurid crypt after the conqueror's death on the warpath to China in 1405. The entrancing blue of its exterior caught the afternoon sun. There were honeycombed stalactites, or *muqarnas*, in its portal. The squarish Kufic script, its hard angles a counterpoint to the floral excesses of the rest of the design, snaked its way up in bright blue over the two minarets. There was nothing in the world that spoke more definitely of Central Asia—a dream of moisture in an arid land—than that tiled blue. I had seen shreds of it in India, but now I felt as if I had come to its source. Timur did not invent the turquoise tile—it came, like all great things Islamic, from Persia—but he made it sing. His artisans cut and carved it; they dressed slim pillars in it and giant domes; they shoved it in squinches and let it unfurl over the spandrels of arches. As Aziz said, "Timur wanted to build in a color that would challenge the sky with its own beauty."

It was odd to think of the sanguinary conqueror at rest under a slab of black jade. His martial spirit had stalked the ages so much so that it was said that if Timur's sleep was ever disturbed, the dogs of war would be loosed upon the earth again. The godless Soviets paid no heed to these superstitions and had him dug up in June 1941. No sooner was he awake, his skeleton being prodded and poked in Moscow, than Stalin learned that Nazi Germany had invaded the USSR.

IN SAMARKAND, I felt a melancholy that followed me west to Bukhara and deepened in Khiva. At Samarkand's Registan Square, I learned of the extent to which the city's buildings, first under the Soviets and later under the Uzbeks, had been unsparingly restored. It was so comprehensive that it utterly obliterated the action of time. Philip Glazebrook, in the 1990s, on seeing something similar in Khiva, asked himself: "But what has renovation, matched colours, taste and tidiness, to do with an Asiatic city? The deadly aim of those weapons has killed Khiva stone dead."

They were words that could not be unread. I had researched old 1960s photographs of tented shops, horse-drawn carriages, and men in white turbans on the main enclosure of the Registan. The tile work crumbled from the Brobdingnagian pylons, but the square was alive. It had all since been swept away. The assiduous spirit of restoration contained an invisible agent, sanitizing and astringent, that hollowed "the East" out of Samarkand's buildings, turning them into mere facades. As a child, I remember my mother's description of traveling to the USSR in 1990 as part of the Indian prime minister's delegation. Those were the last days of the Soviet Union and she encountered empty supermarket shelves and a state of general economic collapse, with teenage girls prostituting themselves for as little as a packet of 555 cigarettes. Moscow especially depressed her, then they came to Uzbekistan, and the mood changed. "You could smell Asia in the air," she said, describing folk songs, food stalls, and outdoor markets. The Soviets had sought to impose homogeneity over the distinctiveness of the different nations that comprised their empire, severing culture from its physical manifestations, yet, here, they had been only partially successful.

Glimmers of an older life were still visible in Samarkand. Not in the heavily restored buildings but in more surprising places. One night, as we—Aziz, Madina, Doniyor, and I—were coming home from dinner, we encountered a wedding procession for two couples. The silence of a deserted street in Samarkand was interrupted by drumbeats and cars honking in tune. Young men in dark suits danced in front, carrying a metal pole with a heart-shaped standard that had been wrapped in sackcloth, doused in kerosene, and set alight. One of the grooms was in a long black-and-gold tunic, the other in white picked out in cerise. The groomsmen would lower the heart of fire and dance around it—half, it seemed, in reverence, half in rapture—while all the time singing in Uzbek: "Yor, yor, yorone." They were cheering the groom on into his new marriage, and these young men, with their ancestral veneration of fire, felt part of an extremely old ritual—an atavism in the true sense of forefather, with its origins in the pre-Islamic worship of fire.

This land of many faiths produced an unstable system of values. Aziz and Madina seemed so much a modern couple, living together, traveling together, sleeping unmarried in the same hotel room. But I realized that under the veneer of modernity, more conservative values prevailed. At the Samarkand Restaurant, with its baroque interiors and loud music, now Turkish and Uzbek, now Persian, Afghan, and Russian, Aziz offered

Madina wine. Her natural sulkiness fell away and she began to tap her manicured fingers to the tune of Glukoza's "Tantsui, Rossiya!": "Dance, Russia! And cry, Europe / For I have the most beautiful ass in the world." When she got up to dance, Aziz grew confidential. "Bukhara society is very conservative," he said. As he spoke to me about the way his relationship with Madina would be judged by his society, I realized that these cities—Samarkand and Bukhara, in particular—had been the equivalent of what places like Singapore and Dubai are today. They had been deeply cosmopolitan, places whose values, aesthetics, and religious beliefs were fluid, defined by the different people who passed through. Earlier, when examining a Central Asian mosque with its stone terrace, wooden pillars, and painted canopy, I asked Aziz if the mosque was quintessentially Central Asian. He seemed puzzled by my question. "Three thousand years ago," he said, "we were invaded by the Persians, so we have something from Persia; fifteen hundred years ago, we were invaded by the Arabs, so we have something from the Arabs; one thousand years ago, we were invaded by the Mongols, so we have something from them. There is no such thing as 'our style.'" Without a trace of the need for historical purity that had spread through so much of the world and was feeding a new populism in places like India and Turkey, Aziz said, "These are cities that would not have existed were it not for the Silk Road."

DRIVING TO BUKHARA, we went through bare sunlit hills, their deep furrows full of shadow. Below was the thin slip of a silver stream, which created islands of dark soil, supporting orchards, vineyards, and reddening mulberries, whose leaves are the food of the silkworm. "We have an expression," Aziz said. "Only mountains can be more beautiful than mountains." The hills grew steeper and were covered in a burnt-blond grass. We were in what I can only imagine were the foothills of the Pamirs, the mountain range beyond which lay Persian-speaking Tajikistan. The winding road was lined with signs that said TANDIR—clay ovens known as tandoor in India—and which, like *comca* (pronounced "somsa"), cousin of the Indian samosa, were only more proof of the many fruits of the Silk Road. At a clearing in the mountains, a market had sprung up. Women in black visors, with brightly colored scarves, velveteen jackets, and baggy trousers, had brought the riches of the hills to be sold. They had sacks of licorice and dried yellow immortal flowers—*Helichrysum arenarium*—which aided digestion. There were sunflower seeds, rhubarb, and ginseng—beige, husky, and loofah-like. There were dried figs and red-berried dog rose.

We reached Bukhara at night. Of all the cities I had been to, and was going to, only Bukhara had the right to call itself Bukhara Sharif—"Bukhara, the noble." This was the emirate where the nineteenth-century explorer Alexander Burnes dismounted his horse and changed his clothes before entering its holy precincts that owed their sanctity to the hundreds of mosques, madrassas, and mausoleums they contained, for "these are the emblems of distinction in the holy city of Bokhara [*sic*] between an infidel and a true believer," he wrote in 1835. We drove through modern streets, lined with emporiums and hotels. The buildings seemed to creep out of one malaise—blockish and socialist—into another, the faux modernity of pasting blue-and-brown glass squares onto the facades of crumbling buildings. This was Aziz, Madina, and Doniyor's hometown. I was dropped on the edge of a depopulated old city of a few thousand and allowed to wander alone through the desolate streets. The town of hundreds of madrassas and caravansaries, and one hundred or so mosques, had been subjected to the only fate worse than Genghis Khan's—tourism. There were hardly any people, save visitors who came in droves to see the storied Silk Road town for themselves. The buildings were mostly hotels, restaurants, or boutiques. I stood at the foot of the twelfth-century Kalyan Minaret, which even the great Mongol had spared from destruction, watching red-colored light play on its varied sand-colored surface. I had grown up in India and known many forms of cultural decay, ruin, and vandalism in my life, but I had never known this willful, state-engineered cleaving of a living culture from its physical embodiment, and the establishment of what Glazebrook calls "the museum-city." The buildings stood, redolent of a certain life—I could almost hear the happy commotion of a caravan town—but, to be in the center of Bukhara was an isolating, solitary experience, like being in an amusement park after closing time.

The city had decayed organically until the 1960s and '70s, when its people were put in modern apartment blocks by the Soviets, who turned the city's buildings into a heavily restored Potemkin village for tourists to visit.

ON MY LAST full day in Uzbekistan, racing through the red desert on the road to Khiva, some 280 miles northwest, I was given a glimpse of those vast blank spaces that lay between the caravan towns of the Silk Road; without them, it was impossible to understand these towns' importance. The Kyzylkum (Red Sand) Desert floated above a sea of natural gas. The earth was covered in a faded green-and-pink shrub called saxaul. An immense pale blue Texas-size sky rose above us. The Oxus River, or Amu Darya, lay in a band of silver to our left, forming the border with the hermit kingdom of Turkmenistan, where the dictator Saparmurat Niyazov (also called Turkmenbashi) renamed the days of the week in honor of himself and his family members. My spirits rose at the sight of this desolation, for it was only with this nullity in mind that one could imagine what it was to see the minarets of Khiva, their blue tiles canceling out the despair of the desert, as light from a lighthouse cancels out the darkness of the sea.

Bukhara lay behind me, distilled into a memory of one sublime building, a Samanid mausoleum, which seemed to tie together all the different strands of Silk Road religion and history. It had been built by the Samanid dynasty around the tenth century at the pinnacle of this region's glory—when men like Avicenna and al-Biruni walked the earth—and it was a miracle, having been buried in sand, that it survived the thirteenth-century onslaught of Genghis Khan. An understated cube, with four sleeping pillars, it stood in isolation in northwestern Bukhara. After the renovated excesses of blue and cyan, and the overworked turquoise tile, the austerity of the Samanid tomb, utterly innocent of the use of color, was as refreshing as an unpainted beam of wood. What it did have, worked over every inch, from entablature to pediment to inset pillar, were raptures of baked brick, creating a varied and intricate surface laden with symbolism.

"Let's start to read it," Aziz said. "It reads like a book." Bukhara was once home to a Buddhist community, part of that two-way traffic of monks and scholars, which would cease after the coming of Islam in the eighth and ninth centuries— its name was drawn from the Sanskrit word for monastery, *vihara*. Aziz pointed at the circles, or chakras, that ran along its pediment. The Uzbek scholar Shamsiddin Kamoliddin saw direct Buddhist references in the mandalas in the two spandrels of the central doorway. I saw them, too. Aziz saw crosses, and fleurs-de-lis, as well as the inverted Zoroastrian triangles indicating good thoughts, good words, good deeds. This was among the oldest Islamic tombs in Central Asia, and it was difficult to think of a more indispensable building. It stood like proof of the many natures of this land of confluence.

In my last hours in Uzbekistan, before catching a flight back to New York, I walked along the ramparts of Khiva's Ichan-Kala, or walled inner town, with Madina. The light faded from the clear desert sky, and though the green domes and blue minarets of Khiva were beautiful, I was beginning to tire of these museum cities. I was glad I had managed to see Aziz's apartment in Bukhara. It was part of a *mikrorayon*, or residential complex, set among acres upon acres of identical communist buildings, where dismal yellow lights came on in cramped windows and little bits of corrugated board held together the gray facades. This was how the great majority of the population of these romantic towns actually lived. No cupolas and courts for them, or shadows in the sand. The apartment, with its furry chocolate-colored rug and its unwashed dishes and a small window in the kitchen, was oppressive. I could see why Madina had done a runner nearly a year before. Moreover, when Aziz confided to me that he was prone to jealous rages, I thought she should run again.

"What is the weather like in London?" she asked.

"Rainy," I replied, and asked her what she had done in Dubai for ten months.

"I work as a hostess in an Italian restaurant," she said. "They specialize in truffles."

Truffles in Dubai, I thought. Here was a fruit of the new Silk Road, if ever there was one!

It was the ingenuity and industry of men who brought rare and precious things to far-flung places that had blazed a network of roads across the spine of Asia. That energy was alive and well. All that had happened was that its course, like the shape-shifting Oxus, had changed. The spirit of the Silk Road, I could now see, was all movement, mercantile and unsentimental. It had no time to pay homage to the relics of what had merely been the easy exchange of goods and ideas. The unforgiving logic of trade had reduced the cities of the old Silk Road—Samarkand, Bukhara, and Khiva—to backwaters. Then, like horsemen of a latter-day apocalypse, came the commissar and the restorer, one robbing these fabled towns of their inner vitality in the name of revolution, the other for the pleasure of tourists. Their outstanding monuments, shells to the glory of past relevance, remained, as did the romance of their names, but the caravans had long since moved on.

A Door onto the Sahara

Morocco

THE SHAMROCK GREEN OF CASABLANCA GRADED INTO A flat plain of beige. From the tarmac itself, I could see the beige run into a towering wall of white—the Atlas Mountains. Edith Wharton, in her 1920 travelogue, *In Morocco*, had felt herself fall under the spell of the Atlas and the desert beyond. "Unknown Africa," she writes, "seems much nearer to Morocco than to the white towns of Tunis and the smiling oases of South Algeria. One feels the nearness of Marrakech at Fez, and at Marrakech that of Timbuctoo."

I felt the nearness not of the Sahara but of Stansted and Orly. The "great nomad camp" of the south—which had once attracted the Tuareg, the West African tribe who had plied the caravan route through the Sahara since at least the fifth century BC and were known as "the blue people" of the desert because of their indigo-dyed robes—was awash with the tourist trash of Europe—the EasyJet set. This was a city where glamorous European families, such as the Agnellis, owned houses, where the name of the garden designer Madison Cox, the widower of Pierre Bergé (Yves Saint Laurent and his partner, Bergé, had fallen in love with Marrakesh in the 1960s) was whispered like a holy name among the demimonde. It was impossible now to smell Timbuktu in Marrakesh. Colonial boundaries and modern tensions—the border with Algeria has been permanently closed since 1994, after a conflict broke out between the two countries—had pushed the desert back. One had to go much farther south, across the Atlas and into the Draa Valley, an 8,900-square-mile oasis that ran along the Algerian border, to get a whiff of that world to which the exchange of goods and ideas—first salt, silver, and slaves, then religion, manuscripts, and notions of kingship—had given an inner cohesion. A Persian friend in New York, a man of taste and refinement, had spoken to me one evening of the Draa. He told me of medieval Islamic libraries in small Saharan towns, of shrines to desert saints and of old Jewish houses.

I wanted badly to go. I was mourning an impression of Arabia that I had received ten years before, while traveling in the Hadhramaut region of Yemen, known for its key position on the incense trade, and researching my first book. I feared that civil war in Yemen in recent years had laid waste to that fairy-tale ideal of crenelated mud-walled cities set in a belt of blue date palm, full of cool and shade. It may be odd to go to one place in search of another, but so much has been lost of late, here in the spread of a homogenizing modernity, there through the destruction of ancient sites in places like

Bamiyan in Afghanistan and Palmyra in Syria. Our time is the enemy of the past, and increasingly I find the wonder of travel lies less in the discovery of new places than in tracing the outline of those that have ceased to exist.

It was a relief to see Monsieur Azzdine—burly, bearded, bespectacled, all flesh and blood, with a chipped-tooth smile and a predilection for Winston cigarettes—materialize out of the speculative haze of a WhatsApp chat. He had come to me as men only can in our time. A year before I met a handsome Moroccan yogi on an Etihad Airways flight to Delhi. We became fast Instagram friends. When I needed a driver to take me south into deepest Morocco, it was he who suggested Azzdine. Soon we were all on a WhatsApp group chat titled "Maroc." Once the recipient of the French prize at college, I now speak an execrable but energetic French, full of unwarranted ambition. When Azzdine expressed fears about *le sable*, I thought, "Le sable?" dimly recollecting the title of a 1985 novel by the great Moroccan writer Tahar Ben Jelloun: *L'Enfant de Sable*. "The Sand Child" . . . *aah* no, I assured Azzdine, it was not the sand of the Sahara I was after, but the *world* of the Sahara. We agreed on a price and arranged to meet at Marrakesh Menara Airport.

We made a brief gas stop at an Afriquia station, then we sped out of the pink city, whose streets were lined with orange trees, their fruit-laden canopies pruned into perfect cubes. I caught flashes of bougainvillea in deep shades of cerise framed against a sky of such intense blue that even the

French Romantic painter Eugène Delacroix, in 1832, had not attempted to paint it until his return to France months later. We ascended into the Atlas, heading southeast via the Tizi n'Tichka, a road renowned for its sweeping vistas and sharp spiraling gradient.

The girdle of the Atlas Mountains that gives Morocco its crooked spine had also served as a barrier of sorts between worlds. The *bled al-makhzen*, the region of law, lay on one side; the *bled al-siba*, literally the "region of anarchy," lay on the other. These were precolonial distinctions that divided the area under the rule of the seventeenth-century Alaouite dynasty from the ungoverned tribal area in the south that had not submitted to its authority. Half this humpbacked country faced the sea, from which the influence of Phoenicia, Carthage, and Rome had washed over it; the other half gazed out at an ocean of sand, no less a world unto itself. Out of the east had come Arabia and Islam, blending with the oldest element in Morocco's syncretic character—the Berbers. These were the Indigenous inhabitants of North Africa who spoke Afroasiatic languages, a world away from Arabic, and who practiced various animist cults. Their history, their language, their dress and customs served as a link to the ancient past of the land, as distinct from the history of the Islamic faith brought about by the successive waves of conquest starting in the seventh century.

"There's no *mere* landscape," J. M. Coetzee said in 2001, firmly putting down an interviewer who wished him to move "beyond questions of mere landscape." In Morocco, I understood the meaning of these words, for the landscape grew so varied that it seemed almost to stand as a kind of shorthand for the country's myriad natures. The ferric red of Central Africa appeared in furrowed hills covered in sparse emerald grass. Ahead, in the same frame, was a Swiss pine forest that led up to high craggy mountains, with peaks of waxy sunlit snow. The burnt shrub-covered hills of a Greek island played host to great stockades of flowering cactuses. Dense clotted argan, dark verdure against dark earth, appeared alongside slim-limbed almond blossoms, their canopies feathered white. The gorges were silvered with lush olive groves that owed their fertility to brawling streams, thin as ribbons. These impossible combinations, this infinite variety—all this, and not any one thing, was Morocco. It felt as if the earth was tearing at its seams, revealing the full range of its possibility, continents colliding into one another, all in anticipation of the nullity and open sky of the desert.

It was evening when the Tizi n'Tichka spat us out onto a road that led down to an arid plain near Ouarzazate—known as "the door to the desert"—120 miles southeast of where I had first landed in Marrakesh. The westering sun penciled the furrows of the red hills. A chill silence spread over the land. This was the likely setting for that most frightening of all of Paul Bowles's stories, "A Distant Episode" (1947), in which a professor, soon to have his tongue cut out, descends from a "high, flat region" at evening toward a "flaming sky in the west" and "sharp mountains." Bowles lived much of his long, louche life in Morocco, where in between parties and rent boys, he received droves of ardent fans from the United States. The late New York painter and poet Rene Ricard visited him in Tangier and told me that as one Moroccan boy more beautiful than the next appeared—now at the petrol station, now at a carpet shop—Bowles would kiss him on the forehead and, turning to Ricard, say, "I used to know his father."

M'HAMID IS THE last town in Morocco before the Algerian border. The road doesn't so much take you there as simply runs into the sand. On the afternoon of the second day, we arrived at a small hotel called Dar Paru. It was the last property along a dirt road lined with mud-brick villages. Paru was a German proprietor who had adopted her Sanskrit name upon becoming a renunciant. She sat outside in the late afternoon sun, an older woman with a shock of white hair, drinking tea and examining a map.

"Have you seen our door to the Sahara?" she said with a strange smile.

WE SAT IN a lush garden of olives and date palms. It seemed inconceivable that the desert could be so close. Paru directed me to a door at the far end of a walled garden. I opened it, and there, in the crude doorframe, was the boundless expanse of crescent dunes edged with sharp black lunettes. It was arresting, unspeakably beautiful, and yet I felt an odd sense of trepidation at finding myself in this empty hotel on the edge of a desolation almost the size of the United States.

"What brought you here?" I asked Paru.

"My inner voice," she replied easily.

Paru then began to speak of the desert fathers and of *marabouts*, holy men who, in these parts, had used the desert as a site of spiritual inquiry. She spoke with intensity of shrines to these men in ancient villages that bordered the Sahara. "They found freedom," Paru said. "They found their spirituality without the Quran, without anything. Just through their insight."

The dictates of Paru's loud "inner voice" had made her leave her husband in Germany in the mid-1990s and come, via Spain, to this place in the desert. Upon seeing the property, she collapsed in tears, overpowered by a feeling of recognition. She recalled panic seizing her on a trip in the desert with the Berbers. Not religious, and certainly not Muslim, she found herself uttering the first part of the Islamic proclamation of faith—*La illaha illa Allah*: "There is no God but Allah"—again and again. She resisted the full formulation, "but," she cried, as if still surprised at how the testament of faith had come to her unwilling lips, "it belongs, doesn't it?"

And so, Paru said the rest—*Muhammad rasul Allah*: "Muhammad is the messenger of Allah"—till her fear was gone. It was as if she had invoked the protection of a monotheistic faith against a holy terror that seemed to emanate out of an older world of pagan worship.

That night, I would know fear of my own. We say we travel to experience, and yet when real experiences come our way, especially those that are not easily explained, the traveler hesitates to record them.

Darkness fell. I ate a tagine of meatballs alone in a firelit room. Paru joined me for dessert, then I retired into a small high-ceilinged room, narrow as a coffin, with a bed draped in a white mosquito net.

At about 1:30 a.m., I awoke in terror. My body was frozen, as if pinned down by an invisible force. Cold spasms ran up my spine. I had trouble breathing and the darkest visions engulfed my mind. I was neither asleep nor awake but in some kind of half state. I tried as best I could to turn my mind to all the positive things in my life, my husband, my dog. Yet all that was good went bad, returning to me in the image of my fear, which was physical and prehensile, like a swarming of nerves. Paru herself appeared to me as a witch doctor, a sorceress. It was then, recalling the story she had told me, that I found myself uttering the same words she had used to ward off her fears: *La illaha illa Allah, Muhammad rasul Allah . . .*

It was the first time in my adult life that I had prayed.

IN THE MORNING, I did not speak of what had occurred the night before to Paru. But I was determined to get away. We spent the morning driving through barley fields, edged by the Sahara. Paru pointed out the squarish shrines with domed ceilings, framed against the ribbed surface of the open desert. The nearness of Timbuktu—still fifty-two days away by camel, one sign read—which was the epicenter of trade and culture on the trans-Saharan caravan route and a fabled name in the Western imagination, was palpable in M'Hamid. I felt I stood at the periphery of an interconnected world of worship and belief.

It was disturbing to think of myself as rational and irreligious but to have an experience that felt supernatural. Nothing remotely close to this had ever happened to me before. I had laughed at those who claimed to see ghosts or be unnerved by the energy of a place. I had no means to understand what happened at Dar Paru, nor did I want to make a place in my life for magic. It was unassimilable, my night in the Sahara, and it left me disquieted and full of doubt. I could not believe, but I would never mock again with so much conviction.

That afternoon, some forty-five miles north, at Tamegroute, a fly-bitten town along a dusty road, I was given a glimpse of the lines of transmission that had once connected the defunct world of the Sahara. Here, where a community of potters still produced the tiles whose manganese green glaze evokes eternal scenes of Morocco and Muslim Spain, and where a few urchins stood around a square, playing at being muezzins with long pieces of piping, Sidi Mohammed ibn Nasir, a religious teacher and physician, had established a Sufi order called the Nasiriyya brotherhood in the seventeenth century. Nasir had made a vast collection of manuscripts redolent of the private libraries of Timbuktu that al-Qaeda-allied fighters tried to destroy in 2013.

The library had closed for a midday break, but Azzdine had the presence of mind to pay a small bribe to one of the local guides. A bit of theater ensued. We were told the guardians of the library—two men, each bearing a different set of keys—were on their way.

"Voilà," cried Azzdine, stubbing out a Winston, at the sight of an old man with thick black sunglasses, Ray Charles in a *djellaba*, who came gliding onto the central square in a wheelchair. He wore a crocheted skull cap of white and gold and a giant hearing aid. This august toothless figure was the senior guardian. He was soon joined by a younger man, who arrived, stage left, on a BMX. The two keepers of the keys opened the doors of the great library in succession, and, seconds later, we were in a treasure house of medieval learning.

"Pythagore!" the old deaf librarian yelled at me, as I gazed vacantly down at an Arabic translation of the Greek mathematician's work. There were works of botany and astronomy, a magnificent medieval Quran inscribed on *peau de gazelle*. The library once held some tens of thousands of manuscripts. That number had declined of late—the works were scattered in museums elsewhere—but the library itself stood as an outpost of learning at the edge of a vast emptiness.

ABSENCES CAN EXERT a gravitational pull. That afternoon, Azzdine and I drove for hours along the circumference of one of the greatest absences known to man. The Sahara, though now out of sight, was behind a line of red mountains—the Jbel Bani, a low, arid mountain range that runs like a seawall on the southern side of the Anti-Atlas—whose striated surfaces formed whorls, as if bearing the impression of enormous thumbprints. The lines brought a feeling of continuity, as did the belt of blue palms. Now and then on the burning plain there would be a single *Acacia raddiana*, a squat, flowering desert tree, its umbrella-shaped canopy casting a tantalizing pool of shade.

In New York, I had heard of a Frenchman called Patrick

Simon, an autodidact with an encyclopedic knowledge of the Draa. I had been trying to track him down for days. The man I found that evening, sitting on the roof of a ravine, on the telephone, a silk scarf around his neck, had lived more lives than are possible to enumerate. Simon, who had been in Morocco for over forty years, had by turns been a decorator, actor, hotelier, and conservationist. He was in his seventies now, a short man with an elfin face and boundless energy. His signature achievement is a geo-park, a conservation area that encompasses 46,300 square miles of the Draa Valley, from Tantan, on the ocean, to Zagora, deep inland.

"If there is one living oasis in the world," said Simon, holding up a flat-palmed hand on which he, a widower, still touchingly wore his wedding ring, "it is this one." He described Morocco itself as a pivot, a place where Europe, Africa, and Arabia coalesce. Tissint, the Draa town nearest to us, where Simon had set up an encampment of brown Bedouin tents, means "salt" in Berber. It was the key commodity in the trade that had stitched together the Sahara. The Berber element had grown stronger as we drove deeper into the Draa, and, racially speaking, we were in a region that was much nearer to sub-Saharan Africa than Arabia. Simon explained that it was the Arabs who had brought the date palm to this region, thus establishing the economy of the oasis, and ensured the spread of Islam.

"Who was here before?" I asked.

"Ancient Jewish, Berber, and Christian communities, as well as animists," Simon answered.

A Jewish community had still been here in Wharton's

time—"Jews abounded in the market-place and also in the town"—working the silver trade and living in ghettos, "into which," Wharton writes, they were "locked at night, as in France and Germany in the Middle Ages." In the postwar years, some quarter of a million had immigrated to Israel, Europe, and America.

Abdel Majid, a spruce Berber youth in his twenties who worked for Simon, promised to show me the *quartiers juifs*, the neighborhoods of small Draa towns where the Jewish community had traditionally worked and lived. Abdel Majid, who switched effortlessly between French, Arabic, and Berber, seemed to carry within him the three-tiered history of Morocco.

It grew dark. The sky was encrusted with thick clusters of stars. Simon opened some white wine and we sat by a fire talking about the tension that exists in Muslim countries between the pre-Islamic and the Islamic past. "The time before Islam," V. S. Naipaul writes in *Among the Believers: An Islamic Journey* (1981), "is a time of blackness: that is part of Muslim theology. History has to serve theology." I had been in Morocco scarcely a few days, and I felt already as if I had entered a sphere of deep atavisms and belonging. It was as if the pre-Islamic Berber past breathed easily next to the Arabized country—and yet the Berber history, old beyond conception, was a source of wonder even to someone like Azzdine, who was married to a Berber woman. People spoke of their Berber roots in Morocco, almost as if speaking of an unknown part of their nature. In the streets of Draa towns, the diptych of Arab and Berber, as Abdel Majid pointed out the next day, was enshrined in the dress of women. The Berbers wore brightly colored skirts, velvety blouses, and headdresses, known in parts as *idgharn*, while the Arab women wore wonderful floral or tie-dyed *imelhafen*, all cut of a single cloth.

Abdel Majid, Azzdine, and I were on our way to see the Jewish quarter in a small Draa town called Akka, eighty miles southwest of Tissint. The delineation of absence had been my theme as I traveled through the Draa, along the perimeter of a void, to which men through the traffic of commerce and thought had brought unity. On my last morning in the Draa, I was granted a glimpse of the empty house of a community that had once formed an integral part of a now-shattered wholeness. There were Jews in Morocco who had come to the country after they were expelled from Catholic Spain in the fifteenth century, but the Jews of the Draa were a far older community, composed of merchants and artisans, with roots in the region that stretched back to at least the second century. Abdel Majid pointed out the small doors that were apparently typical of communities that worked with silver; he showed me the craggy mud-brick buildings and the narrow, shaded streets, now moraines of trash; but none of this spoke to me of the Jews of Akka. Then, by pure chance, we stumbled upon a house whose walls had been torn away. Located above an alcove were shreds of ornamented stucco, now in a T shape, now in a circle. One was covered in tiny circles of blue, white, and brown; the other, in blue almond-shaped leaves against a white background. *What were they, these strange mystical symbols?* They seemed almost to be part of an ancient game board or mandala—so abstract, so suggestive, so moving in their determination to remain as material proof of those who had departed.

THE THEME OF exile and absence followed us to Taroudant, which sat in the shadow of the Atlas, now just a violet outline, 140 miles southwest of Marrakesh. It had been a surreal journey, in which I had let people and experiences come to me, as they would, resisting nothing. And it was to take one last surreal turn. My Persian friend in New York, who had first told me of the Draa, was an intimate of the last empress of Iran, Farah Pahlavi. As I entered my fifth day of being filthy and unshaven, with scarcely a clean T-shirt let alone a jacket or formal shoes, I received a direct message from him: "I was just contacted by H.M. Queen Farah, and she asked you to come to dinner tomorrow."

A discreetly lit blue door led into a pleasure garden where night-blooming jasmine wafted through the night air. In a great room, decorated with candlesticks of dull brass and ostrich eggs in bowls, a fire burned on one end and a floodlit swimming pool was visible through glass doors. A phalanx of silver-framed photographs of the last shah of Iran was arranged along a sideboard. Mohammad Reza Pahlavi and his wife, Farah, had left Iran in 1979 after the Islamic revolution that brought Ayatollah Khomeini to power forced them out. The shah died soon after of cancer, while Farah began a long exile in Egypt, the United States, and Paris. She bought her mud-brick house in Taroudant, where she came several times a year, because it reminded her of the country to which she longed to return. Soon the *shahbanu*-in-exile (*shahbanu*, which means "empress" in Persian, was created expressly for Farah) would appear, still radiant at eighty, with black ribbons in her gold hair and corals on her neck. Soon there would be a wonderful dinner, full of friends and family, where talk would turn inexorably to exile and revolution and elites pushed out of countries that were changing too fast. Soon, over a table laden with Persian rice, the last empress of Iran would turn to me and say, "In exile, food becomes important." Soon Mowgli, Her Majesty's King Charles spaniel, would shower me in kisses. Soon I would be left with an odd feeling of melancholy at having met one of the legendary figures of the twentieth century, this lady who retained an almost girlish sense of innocence and humor, despite having lived through the loss of countries and children, and more experience than several lifetimes could encompass. Soon there would be all this, but before I walked through that door and civilization returned with all its force, I found it hard to let go of the image of that other door to the Sahara in Dar Paru.

My Persian friend in New York had spoken of the persistence of magic in Morocco and of a sphere where the old gods were yet to be overthrown. In Taroudant, I knew I would be leaving this sphere behind me, climbing up into the mountains, back into the bled al-makhzen, the region of law. The world of Islam would return, grafted thinly upon a core of older belief—what Wharton calls the "old stone and animal worship, and all the gross fetichistic [*sic*] beliefs from which Mahomet dreamed of freeing Africa." Even from the great mosque at Tinmel, once the Almohad capital, it would be impossible to reenter the feeling I still had as I stood in that great house on the other side of the Atlas.

It was a feeling of vacancy, of being emptied out by the desert. The silence we had come out of—and which made Azzdine exclaim, "*Le radio enfin,*" as a remix of "Bella Ciao" blared, announcing our arrival in Taroudant—was fading. Variety had returned, erasing the shattering sameness of the plain against which every little tomb and tree was amplified into a focusing point for the eye and the spirit. For one brief moment, I stood in a liminal place. Ahead was a door to a brightly lit room full of laughter and cheer; behind me was Paru's door to the Sahara; and all around me, in my bones, I knew, as perhaps I may never know again, the power of the desert as a spiritual resource. And it frightened me. I had an intimation of the fragility of the bled al-makhzen—the sphere men create to keep at a safe distance the perturbation beyond, should one step through the wrong open door.

The Ghosts of al-Andalus

Spain

ON A MORNING OF HAUNTING HEAT IN SEVILLE, I sought out the tomb of Ferdinand III. There, in the Gothic cool, older Spaniards came and went, dropping to one knee and crossing themselves before the sepulcher of the Castilian monarch. There were men in staid tucked-in shirts, gray checked with yellow, and women with short-cropped hair and knee-length dresses, slim belts around their waists. They sat in pews under a coffered ceiling, dourly communing with El Santo, the patron saint of what would come to be called La Reconquista—the man under whom five and a half centuries of Muslim rule had in 1248 come to an end in this town: Seville, or Ishbiliya, as it was known then.

On a banner above the altar, silver letters against a crimson ground read PER ME REGES REGNANT ("By Me, Kings Reign"). The Virgin of Kings, dressed in orchid pink, gazed down at this scene of historical piety. Black-haired putti, prying and vaguely deviant, swarmed around her. The organ played. Latin chants filled the ribbed recesses of the largest Gothic church in Christendom, which retained as its belfry the fabled minaret (La Giralda, or "weather vane") of the twelfth-century mosque on whose bones it had been built.

It was not merely to escape the murderous heat of that June day—we were in the midst of an *ola de calor* in Andalusia, with temperatures reaching 115 degrees Fahrenheit—that I entered the tomb of Ferdinand III; it was because I wanted to begin my journey through the ghost lands of Muslim Spain by seeing with my own eyes an inscription I had heard about. I looked for it on the sarcophagus of the sainted king, which was partially concealed by the gold of an altar rail. Standing up among the worshippers, I caught a glimpse of what was no less wondrous now in real life than it had been in my reading. There were four plaques in the four languages of medieval Spain—Hebrew, Arabic, Latin, and Castilian—the last of these commemorating the victory of "the great king Don Ferdinand, Lord of Castile, Toledo, León, Galicia, Seville, Córdoba, Murcia, and Jaén" over a land that was soon to become *toda* España to the conquering Christians, Sefarad to the Jews, and al-Andalus to the defeated Muslims.

The plaques marked a Christian victory, but it was not (yet) one that came at the detriment of a plural Spain. The conquering king's son—Alfonso X, El Sabio, or "the Wise"—had grown up steeped in the Arabic culture of al-Andalus. It was only natural that he should feel at home in its different liturgical languages. The plaques used the Hebrew calendar (the twenty-second day of Sivan 5012), the Islamic Hijri (the twentieth day of First Rabia 550), and the Gregorian (May 31, 1252, although history marks his death as the day before) interchangeably, as well as Quranic phrases, such as *radi Allahu anhu*, "may God be pleased with him," to celebrate Ferdinand. But if there was something a little heartbreaking about this familiarity, this ease, this effortless switching between religious cultures as if between selves, it was because this Spain of three natures was on the eve of destruction.

"Remarkable—and poignant," write the authors of *The Arts of Intimacy: Christians, Jews and Muslims in the Making of Castilian Culture* (2008), Jerrilynn D. Dodds, María Rosa Menocal, and Abigail Krasner Balbale, "given that later historical perspective from which we now read them, knowing that Jews and Muslims would be expelled from Spain and from the memory of what had ever constituted the Castilian community—is the use of the place names Sefarad and Andalus to mean Spain." But how does a place so steeped in diversity come unstuck? What makes a society succumb to that primal cry for a *limpieza de sangre*, a "purity of blood"?

Stepping out into the garish day, I stood for a moment at the base of La Giralda—it rose, a broad pitiless mass, some 350 feet into the blue, its summit covered in an enthralling, ever-repeating expanse of *sebka*, a pattern of interlacing multifoil arches (*shabka* means "net" or "ring" in Arabic) in which the play of light and shadow is reduced to a game of inches—considering the history of Islam in Spain.

There are, I want to say, three societies in the world—Spain, the Balkans, and India—that have known this particular kind of history, namely centuries of Muslim rule among large swaths of an unconverted population. Each of these places has experienced periodic cycles of religious violence and ethnic cleansing, whether it was the Balkans in the 1990s or the bitter partition of India in 1947 that left more than a million dead and caused the largest peacetime migration in the history of humanity. What makes Spain unique is that here the aims of ethnic cleansing were fully realized.

There are still Muslims in the Balkans. There are, despite partition, which saw the creation of a predominantly Muslim Pakistan, still 200 million Muslims in India. Spain alone achieved pure erasure. Yet everywhere in this part of Spain, in tangible and intangible ways, we were surrounded by the remains of the Moorish past. They were there in the honey-drenched and cinnamon-dusted pastries (*pestiños*) that the Andalusians ate during Holy Week; there in the Spanish use of *fulano* to mean "so-and-so" (from *fulan*), a version of which we had in India, too; they were there in grand monuments, such as La Giralda or the Mezquita of Córdoba, and the Alhambra in Granada. But they were also there in quiet, unspoken ways, such as in the Alcazar (from *al-qasr*, or "castle") of Carmona (Qarmuna), twenty miles away from Seville. The old Moorish castle sits in the midst of the classic Spanish white town at the crest of a hill of burnt-yellow grass, a brooding presence with its horseshoe-arch entrance and its shattered crenelations. *Shards* is the word historians have used to describe these vestiges, and they exist everywhere—consider how almost one-third of English's vocabulary can be traced to the Norman Conquest of 1066—but what makes them radioactive in Spain is that the heirs to that past were systematically expelled. The silence one feels then, standing in the patio of the church of El Salvador in Seville, where the arches of the old mosque, with their characteristic capitals of Roman *spolia*, are still visible amid mashed oranges lying at the feet of trees laden with fruit, is not natural. It is an enforced silence.

"SEVILLE IS A city of shadows," writes V. S. Pritchett in *The Spanish Temper* (1954), "which tunnel under a dense foliage that is dead still, and pleasure seems to walk with one like a person, when one is alone. There is never too much light." On that first day, walking through narrow streets decked with shadow curtains—*cortinas de sombra*—clinging to an ever-shrinking margin of shade, I was simply dazed by the Saharan heat. I'd spent many summers in the hills above Seville, but I had never known it to be so hot so early in June. In bars, into whose awnings sprinklers had been fitted that released timed bursts of cooling mist, I could make out, through their permanent air of afternoon, wainscotings of *azulejo*—literally "little stones" in Arabic, glazed tiles cut in geometric patterns.

I was in a European town of white buildings picked out in browns, ocher, and burnt umber, trying to imagine its Muslim past, aware that to even think of these categories as mutually exclusive was itself a distortion of history. Spain, like India, had been part of that original Arab expansion when, within a century of the Prophet Muhammad's death in 632, the armies of a new conquering faith reached as far west into Christian Europe as Poitiers in France, where they were defeated by Charles Martel, Charlemagne's grandfather, and as far east as

Hindu Sindh and Multan, in what is today Pakistan. "A hymn to the virtues of exile" is how Menocal describes the history of al-Andalus in her 2002 book, *The Ornament of the World*. It opens with the tale of an exiled Omayyad prince, Abd al-Rahman I, escaping a massacre in Syria, from which he fled to North Africa as his family's sole surviving heir, and founding the Emirate of Córdoba in 756. The Omayyads, who traced their origin to the Mecca of the Prophet Muhammad, were Islam's first dynasty. They had conquered great stretches of the classical world, from Sassanid Persia to Coptic Egypt and the Byzantine Levant. In 711, within a year of the conquest of the western reaches of India, Tariq ibn Ziyad had led a Berber, Syrian, and Yemeni army across the Strait of Gibraltar (also known as Jabal Tariq, Tariq's Mountain), defeating the Visigothic king Roderic. The Visigoths (western Goths) were one of many Germanic tribes who had taken up the mantle of Rome, ruling Spain since the fall of the Western Roman Empire in 476.

Abd al-Rahman I, also known as al-Dakhil, or the Entrant, gave the Omayyads a second lease on life in Spain, even as their power was being smashed throughout the rest of the Islamic world. A new dynasty was on the rise. The Abbasids (of Harun al-Rashid and *Arabian Nights* fame) would go on to replace the Omayyads as caliphs—from *khalifa* in Arabic, "successor" (to Muhammad)—turning Baghdad into the capital of the now-vast Islamic empire. But what makes the history of Islam in Spain read, as W. Somerset Maugham writes in *The Land of the Blessed Virgin: Sketches and Impressions in Andalusia* (1905), "far more like romance than like sober fact," is that it opens with the unlikely establishment of Abd al-Rahman's emirate, which at its apogee in the tenth century would comprise the entirety of Spain, save for the Atlantic North. *Al-Andalus* is the term we give to all of Muslim Spain, its borders expanding and shrinking over the course of eight centuries, political configurations changing, emirates rising and falling. (Andalusia, the province, derives its name from the same word, for it was here in the south that the Islamic presence lasted longest.) The demise of al-Andalus came in 1492, the year Christopher Columbus sailed to America, with Boabdil, the last Muslim ruler of Spain, handing over the keys of Granada to the Catholic monarchs, Isabella I of Castile and Ferdinand II of Aragon. "Don't cry like a woman for what you could not defend like a man," Boabdil's ball-breaker of a mother is said to have told him (no doubt apocryphally), as he cast a teary glance back at the city he would never see again, emitting what my guide at the Alhambra described as *el suspiro del moro*: "the sigh of the Moor."

Spain is a land of churches upon mosques upon churches. This was not new in itself. I had spent months in Damascus, where the Omayyad mosque had been built on the remains of an old Byzantine church that in turn sat on the Temple of Jupiter. In India, I had seen mosques reuse the columns of old temples that filled the imprints of Buddhist viharas. There is nothing more natural (not to mention practical), when conquest is swift and building materials scarce, than to repurpose the sacred to fit the demands of a new time. What was unnerving was the silence of the people who might have been heirs to these ruins. As evening fell and the dome of heat

Aatish Taseer

lifted, I found myself at an opening at the Centro Andaluz de Arte Contemporáneo, an old monastery turned into a ceramics factory that had been converted into a museum. Talking to the vivacious Margot Molina, a former journalist at *El País*, I expressed my interest in the role of al-Andalus in the Muslim imagination.

Her reply reinstated the silence that had been stalking me all day. "But you cannot ask them," she said, "because they're not here."

THE NEXT MORNING, before the heat robbed the day of every trace of freshness, I went to the Alcazar of Seville, built by Peter I (Peter the Cruel) of Castile (1334–69). The great-great-grandson of El Sabio had created what is among the finest examples of an art particular to Spain. Mudéjar—drawn from the Arabic *mudajjan*, "permitted to remain"—refers in the first instance to Muslim populations who chose to stay in cities under Christian rule after La Reconquista. It refers, as well, to an architectural style, one of the glories of this syncretic culture, in which Christian rulers, like Peter I, commissioned Muslim craftsmen to imbue the building techniques and ornamentation of al-Andalus with Christian meaning.

The spirit of those early days of La Reconquista had been assimilative rather than destructive. Alfonso X had styled himself King of the Three Religions and ran a massive translation enterprise out of his capital, Toledo (Tulaytula), transmitting classical Arabic texts on botany, philosophy, law, and medicine across a Europe awakening to renaissance. Well versed in the literary culture of Arabic himself, he would have regarded men such as the Aristotelian theorist Ibn Rushd (born in Córdoba and known to Christendom as Averroes), the Jewish philosopher Maimonides (another Cordovan), and even the great historian Ibn Khaldun, who wrote of civilizational decay, and whose family were from Seville not as foreigners but merely his countrymen. Translation, absorption, reconsecration, getting old stones to say new things—this had been the special genius of medieval Spain, and it was in this tradition that Peter I, who had been in an alliance with the sultan of Granada, built his Alcazar.

Wandering among rooms dripping with muqarnas ("stalactite vaulting") and walls embroidered with arabesques (*ataurique*, from *al-tawriq*), I found myself in the Courtyard of the Maidens. There, against a famous scene of a rectangular pool of greenish water surrounded by multilobed arches, Ahmed, an Egyptian living in Spain, was taking a picture of his mother, who was visiting from Cairo. Birds flew upward into the tent of blue behind the pink of her headscarf. Ahmed was in a structure built by Christians who were celebrating the art of an only recently vanquished Islam. "How did it feel?" I could not help but ask. "The most beautiful," Ahmed said, giving me a smile of tobacco-stained teeth, "the most authentic. We call it a lost paradise." Then, perhaps aware of the oblique angle at which he stood in relation to this work of art, he added, "It's like seeing your own culture from another perspective. It's Islamic, but it's Spanish." The walls were decorated with Arabic inscriptions celebrating Peter I, employing the Granadan creed "There is no Conqueror, save Allah." Ahmed had been trying to read them, but without success. "It's hard," he said. "I don't think it was made by Arabs."

IT WAS THE Spanish philologist Américo Castro who in 1948 first used the term *convivencia* to describe the coexistence of Muslims, Jews, and Christians in medieval Spain—one that inspired many volumes of history that sought to graft the ideals of the secular present onto a medieval past but was met with fierce polemical rejoinders, such as Darío Fernández-Morera's *The Myth of the Andalusian Paradise* (2016). It is probably best, given how treacherous these waters can be, to treat the "ethnoreligious diversity of al-Andalus"—as Brian A. Catlos does in his 2018 book, *Kingdoms of Faith: A New History of Islamic Spain*—less as an "ideal" than as a "fact." It is a *fact* that Jews, Muslims, and Christians, including Mozarabs (from *mustarib*, meaning "Arabized"), lived side by side here for the better part of a thousand years. They intermarried. They participated in a shared intellectual enterprise. They assimilated (and expanded) the art of the Other. They collaborated against their coreligionists when it suited their interests. They each used religion instrumentally, sometimes to be generous, sometimes to be cruel. For some nine hundred years, Spain was a plural society. And then, around the early 1600s, it was not. *What changed?*

It was the question that was uppermost in my mind when I met Miguel Ángel Tabales, fifty-eight, an archaeologist at the University of Seville conducting excavations in and around the Alcazar. He was waiting for me near the exit dressed in a loose blue shirt and sandals.

"You're in the heart of the *taifa* period here," he said as he greeted me, his enthusiasm pushing through his careful, halting English. *Taifa* means "party" or "faction" in Arabic. The Emirate of Córdoba, after a period of *fitna*, or "calamity," in the early eleventh century, fell apart, giving way to a glorious age of city-states, or taifas, of which Seville had by far been the greatest.

Tabales now likened the poet-emir al-Mu'tamid (1069–91) to Rome's Caesar. During his reign, the river Guadalquivir (from *al-wadi al-kabir*, "the great river") had a different position than it does today, making it more conducive to trade. The city grew exponentially, from some 185 acres to 740. "We see it in our investigations," Tabales said. "Each house is the same Islamic house." Yet al-Mu'tamid, in an era of political instability but creative efflorescence, made a catastrophic mistake.

After the fall of Toledo to the Christians in 1085, he lost his nerve and invited the Almoravids, a Berber dynasty who practiced an austere form of Islam, to cross the strait from North Africa and help him drive back the Christian advance. They were happy to oblige, but, after witnessing the chaos of al-Andalus, they returned a few years later, not as allies but as conquerors. Al-Mu'tamid was deposed and became another entry in al-Andalus's catalog of exiles. "Oh, that God might choose that I should die in Seville . . . !" he would write longingly from North Africa. On the way to Tabales's office, I asked about the multilingual inscription on the tomb of

Ferdinand III. "This is very common after the Reconquest," he said. "It gets even stronger in the fourteenth century. When the danger of war was out, the Castilian kings had no problem with minorities. Once they had won, they were more accepting of Muslim influence in the arts"—though not so much, he added pointedly, in politics and religion.

If the early spirit of the Reconquest had been assimilative, by the fifteenth century attitudes began to harden. The Catholic monarchs, Tabales said, referring to Isabella and Ferdinand, "established a political skeleton in which religion was given the first position." One monarchy, one religion became the order of the day, and it was not merely Jews and Muslims who were forced underground.

Arabized Christians had to forsake their Mozarab rite in favor of Roman Catholicism. "It was never easy for the minorities," Tabales said, suggesting that they were ever at the mercy of political calculations. "It's a myth, the convivencia."

As he spoke, I was transfixed by a marble stone, draped in a red cloth, next to the table where we sat. As we were leaving, I asked him about it. He looked at me in astonishment. We were in the stairwell. "But it's the whole history of Seville," he said, insisting we go back upstairs.

The stone, he explained, pointing to a second-century inscription in Latin, had been given by the oil producers of Seville to the goddess Minerva. Under the Visigoths, whom Tabales referred to as "the Germans," it became part of the superstructure of a column in a fifth-century cathedral. With the arrival of the Muslims, it was inverted and made part of a doorway. "The city," Tabales said when we were in the street again, standing under the shred of a Muslim arch, "is full of spolia." But Tabales was not romantic about this use and reuse of old stones. To him, it represented a language of power, of appropriation and reconfiguration. Struggling to recall the Arabic name for it, he said spolia were used to indicate "the upper position of Muslims over Christians."

"If I could go back to any year," said Reyes Abad, forty-four, a researcher in architecture and cultural identity at the University of Seville, "I would go back to 1248," the year the Christians marched into Seville.

She and I were walking home from what was once known as the Gypsy quarter of Triana (Atrayna) on the right bank of the Guadalquivir. Abad, who wore a long dress, had dark Andalusian features and almond-shaped eyes. Earlier, she had made a point of saying that her name was likely Moorish. "Can you imagine," she said, "those Christians coming from the north, which was cold and damp, to what was by then a Muslim city?"

Abad had told me about her doctoral thesis, which addressed the ways in which the architecture of La Reconquista had paralyzed Seville's relationship to modernity. "Seville was the model," she said, "the blueprint for how other cities would look" following the Reconquest. Here, as in other parts of Andalusia, an original period of subsuming and reconfiguring Islamic buildings and using Muslim craftsmen to produce Christian art—like that in the Alcazar—gave way to a triumphalist Renaissance architecture. Abad saw, in its unnatural scale and the rupture it represented, something almost sinister, as if the Reconquistadores were making up in size for the cities they had depopulated. That controlling relationship to buildings, she felt, brought forth a "pedagogical architecture," so that even in the late nineteenth and early twentieth centuries, Seville had been unable to unclench its fist, unable to embrace movements such as art nouveau that were sweeping through other parts of Spain. "We have been a symbolic city for so many years," Abad lamented as we crossed the Guadalquivir.

As we entered Triana—the sun was setting—Abad pointed to an alley leading down to the river: Callejón de la Inquisición. "You can imagine what happened there," she said. "They killed them and threw them into the river."

On Calle Castilla, the Hermandad del Rocío de Triana—one of many brotherhoods associated with the Andalusian pilgrimage of El Rocío—had gathered. There were ancient ladies in floral dresses, with tiny battery-operated fans, and middle-aged men and women, some members of a famous band called Siempre Así. Handsome Andalusian boys threaded a course between them, wearing loafers, collared shirts, and embroidered leather belts. Each, old and young alike, wore a medallion with the coat of arms of the brotherhood on a green ribbon around their necks. An icebox full of wine and beer lay on the ground. When Abad introduced me to our host for what felt like an open house, telling him that I was writing about the legacy of al-Andalus, he grinned and said, "I'm polygamous."

Every now and then a trickle of pilgrims—young girls in beautiful flamenco dresses with shawls around their shoulders, young men in gray hats—would arrive, but the attendees of the nearly four-hundred-year-old pilgrimage, which had been canceled these past two years because of the pandemic, were in for another disappointment. The heat was such that the pilgrims' wagons had been diverted. The main chariot carrying the Virgin would still pass through, but the drama of pilgrims following in its wake would not now occur. The others were more disappointed than I was. I found it incredibly moving to see the arrival of that silver chariot all lit up with white lights. The singing, the cries of "*viva*," the tolling of bells. Then it was over, and the street, so full of commotion and anticipation moments before, emptied within minutes.

"We didn't destroy what we inherited," Abad had said to me. "We changed the symbolism, the language." In fact, as had so often been true in Spain, both things occurred. Just as the Muslims had absorbed and reconsecrated the keyhole arch of the Visigoths and destroyed the Basilica of San Vicente in order to build their Mezquita, so, too, did the conquering Christians absorb what had gone before while proclaiming their victory through acts of destruction.

Abad wanted me to meet Fátima Roldán Castro, a professor of Arab and Islamic studies at the University of Seville. "One of her subjects," Abad texted me, "is discourses of alterity."

"Alterity," Roldán Castro said on my last day in Seville—I was about to catch the train to Córdoba—"was an acknowledgment of difference." It stood in contrast to *otredad*, or "otherness," which she said "could be not very nice."

We sat in a cafe outside the University of Seville, set in an old tobacco factory with a sweeping neoclassical facade. Roldán

Castro wore a green beaded necklace, yellow sunglasses, pink lipstick, and a long black dress. In telling me of the deep influence of Moorish culture on Spain—the use of almonds in food; four thousand loan words from Arabic, such as *aceite*, "oil" (which comes from *az-zait*), or *ojalá*, "God willing" (from *law sha' Allah*)—she focused on how the fall of Granada in 1492 had coincided with Columbus's voyage to the Americas.

"A new world was beginning," Roldán Castro said. "It was necessary to make a Catholic Spain without Muslims," adding what I had heard others say, too: "It was a deal." Which is to say, it was born out of expediency, rather than religious passion.

It was Roldán Castro who first told me about Aljamiado, the secret language of the Moriscos—Muslims forcibly converted to Christianity. Catlos defines *Morisco* as "Muslim-ish." Isabella and Ferdinand had given their Jewish and Muslim subjects an ultimatum: convert or be expelled. Many chose conversion, Jews becoming *conversos*, Muslims Moriscos.

But if there was one great lesson to be drawn from the history of al-Andalus, it was this: when a majoritarian atmosphere takes hold in a society, as it most surely had in Spain, no concession is ever enough. The conversions of the Jews and Muslims to Christianity only excited fears of bad faith.

From those fears came the Inquisition, ushering in an era of book burnings, autos-da-fé, and crypto-identities. What makes it so painful is that these were the same people, with a shared culture, and Aljamiado, for all the suspicion it aroused, was—like Urdu in India, which uses a Sanskritic grammar with a Perso-Arabic vocabulary and script—simply a Romance language written in the Arabic script.

Roldán Castro spoke to me of Mudéjar art, which she described as an artistic language emerging out of a Christian fascination with the legacy of al-Andalus. "I don't know of another place," she said, referring to the singular phenomenon of victorious Christians continuing to work in the creative medium of a now-vanquished Islam, "where a culture keeps on being alive, but with a different mentality, in the Middle Ages," adding that something similar did occur in Sicily, but perhaps not in quite so striking a fashion. If al-Andalus was a place of longing in the Muslim imagination, its place in the Spanish imagination alternated between fetishization and a willful forgetting. This was, after all, still a country where a close friend who grew up in a village in Andalusia remembered his school friends saying, "*Los moros para el otro lado del estrecho*" ("Moors to the other side of the strait").

As Roldán Castro spoke, an uncomfortable thought occurred to me: Was it easier to embrace the art and culture of a people one had subjugated, or expelled? In the United States, there had been no contradiction between enslaving Black people and embracing so much of their culture, from music and dress to food and language. When I asked Roldán Castro if the absence of Muslims in Spain made it easier to adopt their art and culture, she said, "It's a very difficult question. It's not only about religion, it's about any way in which your neighbor might be different from you."

QURTUBA! THERE ARE few names that exert more power over the Islamic imagination than the Arabic word for Córdoba. It was here, at the mosque Abd al-Rahman I first conceived, that the poet Allama Iqbal—the spiritual founder of Pakistan—was inspired in the early twentieth century to sing his lament among these "enduring foundations, these columns without count" for the lost emirate of al-Andalus and for "the upheaval raging in the Muslim soul: that godly secret which dare not find utterance."

I had been here eighteen years before, to this "white and taciturn" city, as Maugham described it, with its stately Roman bridge, where the writer had been "astonished to meet people in European dress rather than Arabs, in shuffling yellow slippers." I had come specifically to see the Mezquita but found it closed. I took it as a sign and went away. In the two decades that elapsed, the building grew and expanded in my imagination. I saw images of what some have described as a forest of eight hundred–odd columns, with their double arches, resembling Roman aqueducts, the alternating voussoirs in burnt red and cream. I read of the bishop who, in the sixteenth century, three hundred years after the mosque had already been converted into a church, planted a Renaissance cathedral squarely within its confines, drawing from his king—the Holy Roman Emperor Charles V (Carlos I of Spain)—the most withering of all reprimands: "You have built here what you, or anyone else, might have built anywhere; to do so, you have destroyed what was unique in the world."

Córdoba itself had become laden with meaning for me. If, as Maugham writes, half the charm of Andalusia lies "in what you divine rather than what you see," I divined the ninth-century poet-musician Ziryab walking these streets, coming from the

Abbasid court in Baghdad to teach the plebes out west about everything from the latest Persian hairstyles to how to eat one's dinner in courses. I divined blue-eyed Abd al-Rahman III, who was three-fourths Spanish Basque, staking claim to the title of caliph in 929, gazing out from his palatine complex, Madinat al-Zahra, on a hill four miles away. I divined that fabled, perhaps imaginary, fountain of mercury on its rolling base that flashed silver for guest after astonished guest. The city that had started as a mere outpost in the eighth century, a cutting from the felled Omayyad tree propagated on foreign soil, had two centuries later grown into one of the premier cities of Islam.

No amount of Google image searching prepares you for that first arresting glimpse, at the Mezquita, of the horseshoe arch picked out in umber and draped in arabesques, a symbol of one culture fertilizing another. It stopped me in my tracks, the sight of it embedded into that outer wall of honeyed stone. I had been in mosque after mosque, from Indonesia to Morocco, but this felt utterly new in inspiration and conception—it felt, odd as it is to say it, European. I stumbled into the cool of a sea of arches, imagining the right-and-left movement of the Islamic prayer that would send them dancing. I wandered through Mudéjar chapels and stood before the strange spectacle of a Christ crowned by interlacing polylobed arches in Pompeian red and white. I came at last to that famous mihrab, whose ribbed ceiling of gold and large-leaved foliage, like a dream of verdure in the desert, returned me instantly to the Omayyad mosque in Damascus. Here was an Islam hungry for the material world, bolstering its spiritual message with new influences, now Greek mosaics, now

Roman engineering. As Hindu numerals traveled west, the Persian dome traveled east, and Islam became like a petri dish for the cross-fertilization of the classical world.

Outside this church upon a mosque upon a church, a pot-bellied Arab sat on the steps, conspicuously reciting his Quran. Beyond was the belfry of the cathedral, in which the minaret of the old mosque had been buried. Many over the years have confirmed the view of Charles V. The church has been de-scribed as a "pustule," and there is little denying that while it is ordinary, the mosque is extraordinary. But I have to confess, I quite like the discordant note it strikes, what Richard Fletcher in *Moorish Spain* (1993) describes as "architectural evidence of strife." For me it felt like a civilizational equivalent of the New York therapist's maxim: "Where there is hysteria, there is history." It was especially poignant, given my upbringing in India. Even as I write, a temple is rising in Ayodhya, in the northeastern state of Uttar Pradesh, on the ruins of a sixteenth-century mosque that was destroyed in 1992 by fanatics who claimed it had been built on the birthplace of the Hindu god Ram. The Mezquita is a reminder of what the wounds of history can drive men to, but it is also proof of hysteria wearing itself out, of people moving on, of the past growing cold.

FIVE HUNDRED YEARS after the fall of Granada, the last emirate of al-Andalus, a mosque had risen in the city in 2003—the first to be constructed in Spain since La Reconquista of 1492. It overlooked the white Moorish neighborhood of Albaicín falling at its feet like a petticoat. The heat, the solemn shape of cypresses, the new mosque on that old stage: it was all very suggestive. Spain now had a Muslim population of 2.25 million people, the majority of them North African. The ancient drama of the coexistence of Christianity and Islam on the Iberian Peninsula was beginning again.

Moments before, I had seen the legendary door through which Boabdil had left. My guide at the Alhambra had spoken of how he had asked Isabella and Ferdinand to seal it shut in perpetuity. The Catholic monarchs honored this most minor clause in the terms of surrender but betrayed Boabdil in more significant ways, especially regarding the assurance that Muslims would be allowed to practice their faith. That assurance was a restating of the ancient Islamic code upon which the plurality of al-Andalus had been founded. Dhimmis, or protected peoples, non-Muslims, had been allowed under Islam to follow their religion unmolested so long as they acknowledged the superiority of Muslims and paid taxes. That law had been in force during the early centuries of La Reconquista, too. But as a new Catholic Spain asserted itself, a creed of uniformity became the order of the day, the old diversity regarded almost as a contaminant. Within a few years of the fall of Granada, the Inquisition came to town. There were public bonfires of Arabic books. Morisco revolts ensued, and more restrictions followed.

To destroy a people, one has first to dehumanize them. One has to tell them they are nothing, that their history and culture are nothing. The final order of expulsion did not come until the early seventeenth century, when tensions between the Spaniards and the Ottomans were high, and Spain's then-diminished

Muslims more suspect than ever. It came after the book burn-ings, the forced conversions, the demands upon a people that they erase every aspect of their identity only to find their tor-mentors questing after further proof of their sincerity, almost as if the very same people who had created this world of shad-ows were now afraid of them. No amount of historical mem-ory could save the Moriscos. All those centuries of intimacy, of living cheek by jowl, of building a shared culture, mattered not a jot. The history of al-Andalus, like that of Germany in the 1930s, reminds us how feeble a protection cultural assimilation is against the primordial scream for a *limpieza de sangre*.

Spain itself, after the bitter civil war of the 1930s, which left some 350,000 dead, had succumbed to Falangism, the fascism of General Francisco Franco. The nearly four-decade dictatorship of El Caudillo—a title drawn from Spain's con-quistador past meaning "warlord" or "strongman"—was an anachronism born out of the nostalgia for empire. The close air of religion and militarism that characterized Franco's rule produced a deep desire for modernity in Spain. The country, like an unfinished picture under a curtain, developed even as the dictatorship remained. When, at last, it fell with his death, in 1975, the Spain that emerged (the Spain in which I found myself) was so ready to be part of the spirit of liber-alism that prevails in the European Union that it is easy to forget it joined the EU only in 1986. The unresolved pain of the Franco years is part of living memory and still not fully processed. In 2019, his remains were removed from his mau-soleum in the Valley of the Fallen and reburied in a cemetery in Madrid; and, in an irony spanning the centuries, the year before my visit, the last statue of El Caudillo was taken down in the North African Spanish exclave of Melilla.

In Las Alpujarras, the mountainous region an hour's drive south of Granada to which the last Moriscos of al-Andalus had fled, there is now a community of Muslim converts and their families. When I asked one of its residents—Medina Tenour Whiteman, a half-American, half-British forty-year-old—what had brought her parents to Granada, where she was born, she said, "They had gone because there was this whole dream of reviving Islam in Europe."

Whiteman grew up in Britain, feeling, she said, very much the "alien, the weirdo," struggling with how being the Muslim daughter of converts in Britain meant engaging in what felt to her like a form of "dress-up," using Arab or Pakistani culture to legitimize her Muslim-ness. In Spain, there was none of that. The memory of an autonomous European Islam still ran in the marrow. What she loved about living here was what she had loved about visiting Bosnia, too: "I can be exactly as I am."

Whiteman, who has written guidebooks and travel guides for Muslims in Spain, had met a man from the province of Extremadura in the west who still recalled his grandmother going to the basement of her house and praying in the Islamic manner, with no conscious awareness that the washing and kneeling were part of Muslim ritual. "The Muslims they were getting rid of," Whiteman said, speaking of the expulsions of the early seventeenth century, were not Arabs or Berbers but "indistinguishable from the Christians carrying it out." The narrative of the Reconquest had been applied centuries later to what she saw as a simple act of ethnic cleansing.

When I asked Whiteman about what al-Andalus meant to Muslims, she said, "We can't help but be aware that something extraordinary took place here. A flourishing—of the word, of knowledge."

At the same time, she was wary about growing too attached to that history. She had prayed the Friday before at the Granada mosque. It was magical, performing the stations of Islamic prayer as the sun sank behind the Alhambra, yet, like all magical things, it was also a little unreal. The Quran, Whiteman said, urges you to celebrate the wonder of the natural world. "It doesn't say, 'Go and look at beautiful mosques and palaces,' so there is a part of us that gets a little fixated on the vestiges of Muslim power," she said.

Those vestiges are what brought her back to Spain, so that she could raise her children in a land where, despite the expulsion of its Muslim (and Jewish) inhabitants, Islam was in the soil, and where she could be part of a pluralistic community, with people to relate to and pray with. "Me in my garden," she said, "tending to my tomatoes is just as Muslim as visiting the Mezquita in Córdoba."

There was something wistful in hearing her, against the backdrop of this now-pacified theater of religious strife, voice a desire for faith to remain a private matter. The Spanish Inquisition, deeply modern in texture and feel, abolished the very idea of the inner life. It gave us the blueprint for what would serve as the dread apparatus of state surveillance ever after. Even so, the Inquisition's dream of homogeneity, it turns out, was no less a fantasy than the imperishable diversity of al-Andalus.

Against the Grain

Mexico

I ARRIVED IN OAXACA ON A RAINY AFTERNOON IN MAY. We flew over pleated hills that formed a girdle around the Oaxaca Valley, one of the most fertile variegated soils in the world. The earth was stamped with cloud shadows that gave an impression both of movement and fixity—a rich, dark earth with an inner seam that showed red and metallic in places. The shadow of the plane, like a fighter escort, followed us as we descended, then was subsumed by the rain-drenched tarmac. The sky was full of light. Leaving the small white airport, we passed a palisade of organ pipe cactuses.

There was blue-leaved agave in the traffic islands and, lining the streets, the trees of my childhood in Delhi—flamboyant, laburnum, jacaranda—were in flower. A nondescript modern town of brightly shuttered shops, auto mechanics, and signs that read ALUMINIO Y VIDRIO gave way to a fully intact Spanish colonial town from the sixteenth century. "Downtown:

local people," my driver said, observing the change, "*centro histórico* for foreign people."

We came along large-stoned cobbled streets and single-story buildings painted in warm shades of ocher and that famous Oaxacan color—a carmine, drawn from the cochineal, a cactus-dwelling insect, which, with the addition of a single drop of lemon juice, turns into one of the most seductive reds known to man. There is no place, not even India, where the use of color produces as beguiling a mixture of gaiety and melancholy as Mexico. The British writer Rebecca West, who was here in the 1960s, has a description in *Survivors in Mexico* (2003) that cannot be bettered: "Here these walls are painted colors that are special to Mexico, touching variants of periwinkle blue, a faded acid pink, the terra-cotta one has seen on Greek vases, a tear-stained elegiac green."

There is a green stone of otherworldly beauty known simply as *cantera* that is everywhere in Oaxaca. It appears as exposed quoins on the corners of painted facades. It forms the border of giant grill windows, which, Spanish-style, run the full length of the building. It is there as rustication and entablature—there, too, on one of the city's main churches, Santo Domingo de Guzmán. On that first evening, I thought my eyes were deceiving me. The sky had turned half a dozen shades of pink and orange before grading into darkness. I walked among captivating scenes of city life—through a first-floor window, there were girls out of a Degas painting practicing ballet.

Opposite was a *mezcaleria* with grizzled old men smoking outside. There were baroque theaters and stooped white saints in the tiny alcoves that appeared on high cornerstones. Outside Origen, which belongs to the renowned Oaxacan chef Rodolfo Castellanos—who still works in his restaurant—I pulled out my phone to inspect the exterior. It was not bewitchment, or blindness; it was that tender, mournful green.

Inside, in a grand courtyard, hung with dried maize whose twirling husks cast starry shadows over the whitewash, itself marked with the Jesuit monogram *IHS*, symbolizing Christ, I ate fried *chapulines* (grasshoppers) as a cocktail snack. A line from Hugh Thomas's *Conquest: Montezuma, Cortes, and the Fall of Old Mexico*, his 1993 history of the subjugation of this land by the Spanish five centuries ago, returned to me. "Almost everything which moved was eaten," he wrote of pre-Columbian Mexico. Then, as a tasting menu of several courses unfolded, each bringing with it flavors that were utterly new, I felt intimations of that pre-Columbian past.

We speak so easily of earthiness, of terroir and rusticity, but we do not know the meaning of these words until we come to Mexico. In *chintextle*—a paste made from pasilla chile—that had been smeared onto a tostada of blue corn, I could taste the flavors of the deep earth. It was there again, that volcanic smokiness, in the mole *manchamanteles*, which, smothering a duck breast, was as red as the soil I had seen from the airplane. Death, smoke, desiccation. It was there, too, in the purée of mangrove mussels upon which a piece of striped sea bass appeared. It was as if a portal had been opened to an underworld from which the savor of Mictlan itself (Hades to the Aztecs) flowed out, endowing everything with chthonic force. I half-thought I was losing my mind until a few days later, when Olga Cabrera Oropeza—the chef and founder of Tierra del Sol, a restaurant specializing in moles—confirmed the feeling I had had on that first night in Oaxaca. "For me," she said, on a terrace with sweeping views of the emerald city, "a mole is the presence of dead ingredients that bring a dish to life." These were pre-Hispanic ingredients—old Aztec flavors, one imagined—many new to me in texture and taste, and, as such, they felt like an emanation of the culinary history of the land.

I had come to Mexico in search of what was perhaps the quintessential post-Hispanic ingredient—rice—and, almost immediately, I was confronted by the most reasonable question in the world: "*¿Por qué arroz?*" ("Why rice?"), asked Eduardo "Lalo" Ángeles, an artisanal mezcal maker with rugged features and sun-scorched skin. Why, in this birthplace of corn, Lalo wanted to know, was I bothering myself about rice? Speaking to me through my guide—Omar Alonso, who sat next to Lalo in a cap for Guerreros de Oaxaca, the local baseball team, under a mural of Mayahuel, the Aztec goddess of maguey (agave)—I heard, in the easy torrent of his Spanish, the word *Chino*. Omar looked slightly embarrassed, then translated: "We're not Asian."

Lalo's surprise piqued my interest. Rice had come to Mexico shortly after the Spanish conquest of the 1520s. It was a time when Spain and Portugal were spreading their tentacles across the globe: the Portuguese viceroy Afonso de Albuquerque's conquest of Goa, on the west coast of India, occurred nine years before the conquistador Hernán Cortés's 1519 march on Mexico. Some four decades later, Spanish vessels known as the Manila galleons first brought rice to Mexico from the Philippines. What interested me was what place this Old World staple, come via Asia through Europe to the New World, held in the lives of these people who had a mythical attachment to corn. Was it an assimilated part of Mexican food, all memory of its origins forgotten, or was it in some ways still a symbol of the conquest? We assume from a certain kind of Mexican food—the rice-filled tummy of a burrito or the red rice that comes with almost every takeout order—that rice is integral to the cuisine of this country. But the numbers tell a different story: per capita consumption may have increased in recent years—from thirteen pounds in 2011 to almost twenty in 2017—but the average Mexican still consumes only one-fifth as much rice as his coeval in next-door Belize. Mexico does grow some of its own rice for domestic consumption, but the majority of its needs, about 70 percent, are met by imports, mostly from the United States. My interest in the role of rice in Mexico could not be reduced to anything so vulgar as bushels. What intrigued me was the relationship of this grain to the cuisine of this great culinary nation—and what, in turn, that could tell me about Mexico's relationship to its difficult history.

To get to Lalo, Omar and I had driven an hour south from Oaxaca to the small distillery town of Santa Catarina Minas, set among serried fields of thorn-edged maguey, a squat, pot-bellied plant with fleshy leaves of a tantalizing aquatic green. Above Omar and Lalo, both in their forties, the goddess Mayahuel appeared bare-chested, between two fronds of maguey, gazing dreamily into the distance. All around me were reddish-black piles of timber and fermenting casks of agave. On their surface, amid clouds of insects attracted to the cloying sweetness of sugar turning to alcohol, Lalo had planted tiny bamboo crosses, a mark of his devout Catholicism. Reflecting further on the question—"*¿Por qué arroz?*"—he said that from his experience, he found that rice was consumed most in places where the church's influence was strongest.

"What's the connection between the church and rice?" I asked Lalo.

"It's an influence from Europe," he said easily, reminding me of how exotic rice could still seem in Mexico even five hundred years after the Old World's "discovery" of the Americas.

Catholicism—like rice and the knowledge of distillation, which made Lalo's mezcal possible—had come with the Spanish conquest. That tale of Cortés, the rogue conquistador, who, having burned his boats, subdued the mighty lake-bound capital of the Aztecs, Tenochtitlan—with its two hundred thousand inhabitants, bigger than any city in Europe, save perhaps Paris—is among the most painful and pitiable episodes in history. With growing horror, one reads of that terrible sequence of events: the first meeting of Cortés and the Aztec emperor Montezuma, one driven by his greed for gold, the other, it was believed by some was laboring under a prophecy that the conquistador was the god Quetzalcoatl, reincarnated; the ninety-three-day siege of the lacustrine city, known as the Venice of the New World, which would leave it a burning ruin; the plague-weakened Aztecs, fatally susceptible to Old World diseases such as small pox, succumbing to the first use of horse and cannon against them. The Spanish triumph, of course, yet one is left feeling a great sense of unease at their victory. As the British neurologist Oliver Sacks wrote in his *Oaxaca Journal* (2002), when confronted by the sheer rapacity of the Spanish melting down of thousands of pre-Columbian gold artifacts at the ruin of Monte Albán, in the hills above Oaxaca, "the conquistadors had showed themselves to be far baser, far less civilized, than the culture they overthrew." Within half a century of the conquest, Sacks writes, the Aztec population of 15 million had been reduced to a subjugated 3 million.

It was during this same period that the Spanish brought rice from Asia, via the port of Acapulco, one of the oldest in Mexico, to their new colony, where the soil and climate were suitable for its cultivation. This movement of goods and technology, by which the Old and New Worlds literally seeded one another, is known as the Columbian Exchange, which had started decades before in Spanish colonies in the Caribbean—including Cuba, Hispaniola, and Puerto Rico—but which had been taken to new heights after the conquest of Mexico. To the Old World there flowed such indispensable things as maize, chocolate, chiles, tomatoes, avocados, potatoes, and rubber. The Americas, in turn, received the wheel, the horse, sugar, wheat, livestock, a syllabic script, and, of course, rice. The changes the Columbian Exchange wrought are so profound, so embedded now in our way of life, that it is hard to imagine the world before them. It boggles the mind to think of India, where I grew up, as not having chiles until only five centuries ago. Or Italy and Greece doing without tomatoes. As the Mexican writer Octavio Paz, who had served as ambassador to India, puts it in *Itinerary: An Intellectual Journey* (1980): "The discovery of America initiated the planet's unification."

But, as we already know, the conquest of Mexico was not a benign affair. Here there was no mere happy exchange of exotic fruit. It left a layered society, full of unresolved historical pain. "The nations of ancient Mexico," Paz writes, "lived in constant war, one against the other, but it was only with the arrival of the Spaniards that they really faced the other, that is, a civilization different from their own." That sentence, mutatis mutandis, could have been written about India, where Islamic invasions and British rule still produced an anxiety about authenticity—what was one's own, what had come from outside. I was interested in that anxiety, which could manifest itself both in tangible and intangible ways.

"*¿Por qué arroz?*" indeed. I guess I hoped rice, like dye in a chemistry experiment, would serve me as a flow tracer of sorts—a way to enter the complexities of Mexico's past through something as concrete as food.

"Rice is not filling," Lalo said. "If you eat it, then after two or three hours in the fields you're hungry again. If you have beans, you can hang on longer."

Omar laughed, in part, I thought, because Lalo seemed to take the intrusion of the crop in his birthplace so personally.

"Think about it," Lalo said. "When was the last time you cooked rice in your house?"

Omar nodded. "It's a restaurant thing."

"But horchata? All the time."

Lalo and Omar spoke to an element of novelty that rice still possesses in this part of Mexico, its tapered southern end surrounded by rice-producing states such as Tabasco, Campeche, and Veracruz. The presence of the crop was remarkable enough for Lalo to associate it with the church, which was inseparable from the conquest. Omar linked it to the more artificial setting of a restaurant, as opposed to what one made at home, reminding me that this was one of those countries, like India and China, where restaurant food was a cuisine apart from what one ate in people's houses. And later, I would meet another chef who would trace its origins in her life to a government food security scheme. All of which is to say that rice, though partially assimilated, still felt somehow alien. (To give you a sense of the disparity: in 2018, Mexico consumed a paltry 1.2 million metric tons of rice, whereas a rice-eating nation of roughly equal size, like Japan, say, consumed over 7 million.) But as the basis for horchata, it was perfectly natural. The drink—a cold, cloudy, sweet liquid exalted by the presence of fruits and nuts—has an ancient origin in North Africa. It came to the Iberian Peninsula via the Moorish conquest of Spain in the eighth century.

Known then, too, for its cooling quality, it was made with tigernuts, but when these failed to make it aboard the ships of conquistadors, horchata was reborn in the New World, with a new basis in rice, still carrying on the fight against the stultifying heat of a day like today.

Before our trip to the distillery, Omar and I had been in the tiny Oaxacan village of Santo Tomás Jalieza, a place of large-leaved verdure, corrugated steel fencing, and tropical lanes of red earth, with puddles that reflected the vacant intensity of the Mexican sky. There, at the house of the Navarro sisters, three unmarried weavers in their fifties, Omar and I had witnessed a rarity even in Mexico: horchata made from scratch. In a shaded courtyard overgrown with succulents, Margarita, with her graying pigtails and brightly embroidered apron, had crushed rice, which had been soaking for an hour or so, on a metate, a hollowed, mortarlike stone. Nearby, Inés, stouter but dressed similarly—in a brown dress and apron, on which sprawled bright blue and red flowers—prepared all that would go into the horchata: melon, walnut, red-fleshed prickly pear. Back and forth Margarita went, mashing the rice to gruel. Now and then she flicked bits of cinnamon onto the pocked ashen surface of the metate. The mashed rice turned a pale brown. When enough had collected in the clay pot at the edge of the quern, the two sisters—the third Navarro sister, Crispina, was an amused bystander—squeezed out its impurities using a wet cloth. Margarita added sugar, ice, and all the condiments. In a round-bottomed gourd, beautifully painted with a bright red ground covered in leaves and flowers, the hemisphere bifurcated by a white-flecked band of superb Mexican blue, which in turn sat on a glazed clay cup, I was presented my first horchata.

On that hot afternoon, the throbbing blue tent of sky above me, it was magically refreshing, full of surprise and fragrance, the drab, ice-cold graininess of its texture transformed by the inclusion of bright fruits and the gritty richness of nuts. It was also a million miles away from any previous notion I'd had of rice. It felt like what in artistic circles is described as a response—as if the New World, desperately bored by the prospect of rice, had souped it up with every possible bell and whistle, so that almost nothing remained of the interloping grain that had tried to muscle its way over to the Americas on the boats of the conquistadors. I drank it down, then drank another.

Swimming back into myself, I saw Omar and Lalo sitting against the turmeric-colored wall where Mayahuel held sway. Thinking of India, where the old gods, despite centuries of conquest, had not been overthrown, I wondered if it was easy for Lalo to balance his regard for the Aztec pantheon with his allegiance to the church.

"For us, no," he said, without so much as a glance back at Mayahuel, whose smoky nectar we had been consuming in voluminous quantities, "because we are the product of the conquest."

THE NEXT DAY, under the "blue uneasy alkaline sky" of D. H. Lawrence's *Mornings in Mexico* (1927), Omar and I, at the Mercado de Abastos—a warren of shaded lanes, no wider than corridors, with sleek, undulating walls of corrugated steel and workman tables dressed brightly in their oilcloths— walked among the ingredients I had tasted that first night in Oaxaca at Origen. As I'd learned the day before, the pre- conquest past, in areas such as language (Nahuatl), religion (an earth religion where the obsidian knife was routinely used in human sacrifice), dress ("the upper class," writes Thomas in *Conquest*, wore robes of long quetzal feathers, and very elaborate cloaks of white duck feathers, embroidered skirts, and necklaces with radiating pendants), and architecture (great stepped pyramids rising out of a lake encircled by volcanoes), has all but gone under in Mexico. But if there is one point of contact, one aperture through which the Mexico of today can reach out its fingers and touch the Aztec past, it is food. And that past, here at the Mercado de Abastos, through the prevalence of corn, cacao, and chiles—and the absence of rice—could still feel very present.

"I don't like to plan," Omar said waspishly that morning over a *café con piquete*—a coffee with a stinging shot of mezcal—in Enrique Olvera's restaurant Criollo. (Olvera is Mexico's original rock star chef, with such establishments as Pujol in Mexico City and Cosme in New York to his name.) Thanks to Omar, we were served up an impromptu feast. Conchas topped with an even layer of charred corn husk, which I was meant to dunk in my coffee. Rib-eye soup. A taco of beef, chorizo, and *quesillo* (string cheese). Another with *berros* (fragrant greens) and a salsa of chicharrones (fried pork skin). All this, I should add, was merely a prelude to the morning of street food Omar had arranged. Observing me quail at the prospect of more, he plied me sadistically with an *enmolada* whose red mole contained the rarest, most expensive of all chiles: *chilhuacle*—stout, triangular, and of impossible smokiness.

"Oaxappiness!" Omar proclaimed.

And then we were off—Omar playing Ariadne to my Theseus—through a street of prostitutes, preening in the clear morning air, deep into the cool labyrinth of the market.

I had been in markets all my life, in places as far apart as Ouarzazate and Luang Prabang, Samarkand and Kigali, but that was the Old World. Here, in this New World market, one felt the ubiquity of the absence of Old World produce like rice, and my reaction was not unlike that of Columbus himself first setting eyes on the newness of the New World: "I saw neither sheep nor goats nor any other beast"—he writes in his journals—"but I have been here a short time, half a day; yet if there were any I couldn't have failed to see them . . . There were dogs that never barked. All the trees were as different from ours as day from night, and so the fruits, the herbage, the rocks and all things." It was amazing how, on that morning, a sense of New World wonder still prevailed after the passage of five centuries.

Dizzying varieties of chiles rose around me in steep escarpments of roachlike red verging on black. I now knew pasilla and chilhuacle, but did I know that there were two varieties of the latter? And what of other chile varieties such as guajillo, cascabel, *and* morita? Omar was relentless, pressing on through the tented streets scalloped with pools of sunlight. Sometimes he would stop to buy a delicacy, like *huitlacoche*—corn that had sprouted an efflorescence of rich blue fungus. We took the corn smut to Doña Vale, an elderly lady whose memelas—a thick pre-Hispanic tortilla—and salsa of tomatillos had made her a TV star when she was featured on the Netflix series *Street Food*. When we found her, she was in a cerise dress ornamented with black lace, two carmine stones in her ears, flanked by a couple of loutish youths in masks and hoodies, taking selfies. In a gesture of friendship, Omar gave her the smut and we plunged deeper into the market, where a thirty-six-year-old woman named Mago, also famous for her memelas, stood ready to make us our umpteenth breakfast. Young and vivacious, in a green camouflage T-shirt, she threw a couple of *hierba santa* leaves on a hot comal, where they wilted instantly, and began to cook eggs over them. In between cooking for us, Mago pressed tortillas between two sheets of orange plastic on a blue metal press from which the paint flaked. The band Grupo Soñador, known for its Mexican take on the Latin American folk music *cumbia*, played a brassy, jaunty number in the background from a speaker. Omar crushed an avocado onto the wilted leaves, scattering *guaje* seeds on it—a vine grass that grows in the surrounding hills, and from which the word *Oaxaca* itself is derived. All around me, from the sight of a woman, standing in the distance, with strong Indian features and pigtails, a basket of nopales (cactus pads) on her head, to men offering me pulque, a pre-Hispanic drink made from the fermented sap of the maguey, I saw the vestiges of a past that, though worn thin in places, was full of novelty. It was against this newness that rice felt almost like a memory of the Old World—a world elsewhere.

ON MY LAST day in Oaxaca, Omar took me to Levadura de Olla, a restaurant whose name means "the yeast of the cooking pot." It had been started by a twenty-six-year-old chef named Thalia Barrios García, who came from San Mateo Yucutindoo, a village in the Sierra Sur, the hills surrounding Oaxaca.

She was kneading three kinds of maize when we came in. One of the joys of being in Oaxaca, unlike other food capitals, was how close the connection still was between fine cuisine and the traditions with which people had grown up. Thalia's aunts and grandmother had all been cooks. She had learned from them.

A government agency with the acronym CONASUPO— which provided food security to economically disadvantaged areas—had introduced arroz to Thalia's village in the mid-1980s. "Rice is something you eat with tortillas before you go to work in the fields," she said, taking us back to the idea of the staple as a raw source of energy and sustenance in agrarian communities. Lalo had said something similar, but with the opposite meaning: rice, he felt, was poor sustenance; beans were better. But what surprised me, watching her make *arroz rojo* (red rice) and *arroz con frijoles* (rice and beans), was how recent that introduction had been. Lalo had traced a line to the church; Thalia now traced one to a government agency. It made rice seem so foreign, so new, in a way that I could never imagine a Punjabi farmer in North India, consuming a corn roti and spinach on a cold winter morning, ever feeling. Obviously, we in the Old World had assimilated the New World far more unthinkingly than was true in reverse. In a beautiful green glazed pot, which sat on a wood-fired comal, Thalia was blackening a few *chiles costeños*. To these, from a clay *sartén*, or pan, she added the softest, mashiest frijoles I had ever seen, then diluted the mixture with water. It was now a soup of sorts, into which Thalia sprinkled salt, avocado leaves, and, of course, arroz.

It was the best thing I ate in Oaxaca. In its raw, terrestrial graininess, it reminded me of dishes, like dal (lentils) and rice in India, that are pared down to a simplicity so perfect that even the addition of salt can feel like a flourish. Soon, other things arrived: five kinds of tomatoes overlaying a beet purée. Mezcal. Then an offspring of the rain, which now came every afternoon like clockwork—a mole of *chicatanas.*

"Chicatanas?" I asked Omar.

"Flying ants," he replied dryly.

"IN EXILE, FOOD becomes important," the ex-shahbanu of Iran had told me, in Morocco. Mexico, in many ways, is a country exiled from its pre-Hispanic past. As with Iran and the Arab conquest of the seventh century, the pain of what had been lost was still fresh centuries after. Considering the nature of Mexico's "inner conflict," Paz wrote, "I found that it was the result of a historical wound buried in the depths of the past."

On that last night in Oaxaca, the reverberations of that wound came to the surface. I sat on a terrace, overlooking dark cobblestones bathed in yellow streetlight, with a young dancer by the name of Enrique. He had a light beard and fine features, and his slight, slim body vibrated with the historical anger that the conquest could still produce in Mexico. "By the end of the conquest," Enrique said, "the people who had the power were the white people. Even the revolutions were led by white people."

The legacy of that conquest, as Matthew Restall argues

in *When Montezuma Met Cortés: The True Story of the Meeting That Changed History* (2018), was taken up by the United States once Spanish power had failed on the American mainland. In two friezes on the rotunda of the US Capitol building in Washington, DC, a clear parallel is drawn between Montezuma's surrender to Cortés and the Mexican general Santa Anna's surrender to the United States after the Mexican-American War of 1846–48. "Every country has its phantoms," writes Paz, no doubt thinking of the war that cost Mexico half its territory. "France for the Spaniards, Germany for the French, ours have been Spain and the United States." Paz goes on to describe Mexico's neighbor to the north as a reality "so vast and powerful that it borders on myth," producing a relationship on Mexico's end that is "polemical and obsessive." How could it not be? The United States' gaze, even before Trump's talk of Mexicans as rapists and criminals, was corrosive, turning this country, with its rich, layered history, into little more than a brutish source of labor. Enrique himself worked part-time as a farm laborer on a plantation in California that grew not rice but marijuana. And that relationship felt exploitative—as it had been for Omar, who crossed the US border illegally when he was eighteen and lived and worked in Los Angeles restaurants for the next decade.

Enrique, in turn, lived with his own sense of historical unease. He was neither white nor Indigenous. Like over half of Mexico, he was mestizo, of mixed blood, a child of the conquest. He privileged the authenticity of Indigenous Mexico, relaying the crimes of the colonizers but, as he spoke, I was reminded of a moment in *Survivors in Mexico*, when Rebecca

West is confronted with a similar situation with a taxi driver in Mexico City. "The man," she writes, "is not identifying some monstrous invader of his people's lands, as Poles might denounce the Nazi Germans; he is denouncing some of his ancestors for maltreating other of his ancestors, which, as he is both, must lead to schizophrenia."

The emanations of that schizophrenia had been with me throughout my time in Mexico. All my life I had balanced different societies in my head. India, Pakistan, the United Kingdom, and now the United States. The return of history in each of these places, not as a discipline, but as a consuming passion, had caused ructions, some of which I had felt directly. In Pakistan, I had seen my father killed for falling afoul of a religious idea of history; in India, I had seen myself shut out of a new historical purity. In Britain and America, my adoptive homes, I had seen historical nostalgia produce an unconsidered populism whose aims were vague, but whose promptings were clear—the fear of being overrun by immigrants. Behind these historical awakenings was the desire to undo rupture and to be returned to the continuities of a past free of the gaze of outsiders. In Mexico now, from the blissful distance of a bystander, I could see continuity and rupture, insider and outsider, manifest in any number of individuals. I had come among people who had been remade by the Spanish conquest but who had battled within themselves on behalf of a truer, Indigenous Mexico. When I asked Enrique to pick out the people who were Indigenous, he said, "They're not here. They're on the street, begging for money or selling candy, but they're not here. They're somewhere else."

Their absence, symbolizing the loss of old Mexico, was pain. On this epicurean journey in Oaxaca, I had seen food serve as a way for people to commune with that vanquished past. It was a rare line of continuity that ran from the pre-Columbian era into the Mexican present, allowing the society to glimpse a shattered wholeness.

But as much as people suffered on account of their histories, their relationship to food tells a different story, speaking always of our talent for assimilation and absorption. "*¿Por qué arroz?*" Lalo had asked. The answer was plain: the Columbian Exchange was proof like no other of how, when it comes to food, so often the venue of our greatest nativisms, we, as human beings, easily slip the ties of belonging. No man dipping his satay in peanut sauce in Bangkok, or woman eating chicken paprikash in Budapest, or any number of families consuming potatoes across the breadth of Russia, stops for one moment to consider how relatively recently these seminal ingredients have been added to their national cuisines, even if, like Enrique, those same people still bristle from the after-effects of conflicts that are centuries old. We apply the terms *invasive* and *native* to the vegetable kingdom. They are full of resonance for us, but every day, at our dining tables, we set aside our obsession with origins—what is ours, what has come from outside—nourishing ourselves on an endlessly fertile encounter with the Other.

The Purity of the Lotus

Sri Lanka

IN ONE SWIFT MOVEMENT, ASOKA SWUNG HIS MACHETE into the side of a tree and left the hooked blade lodged in its trunk. The Sri Lankan lotus farmer was in his late forties, with dark leathery skin, a graying soul patch, and lips stained red from betel nut. He placed his dumbphone in the tree's branches and gestured to me to remove my shoes. The grass felt like rubber under my feet on that February morning. Mud oozed between my toes. "Pankaja," I murmured to myself, "mud-born." It was one of over forty words for the sacred lotus flower (*Nelumbo nucifera*) in Sanskrit. I rolled my corduroys up to my knees and we began to wade into the lake, which Asoka, whose full name is Y. G. W. Dissinayake, had rented for cultivation. The rising sun suffused the thin mist that hung over the water. We soon stood in several inches of soft mud and murky water, surrounded by a colony of lotuses. There were calyxes of faded pink, others in full bloom, with yellowish-white interiors and petals of tragic translucent brightness, sheltered by broad nodding leaves and curled elliptical buds. Most beguiling of all was the fruiting receptacle. It looked like something a spacecraft might have jettisoned as it breached the earth's atmosphere—a magical cup of unbelievable hardiness in whose waxy surface the bean-like seed of the lotus lay embedded, with the power to fruit even after thousands of years.

Nelumbo—the scientific name for the genus of the sacred flower, first adopted by the French botanist Joseph Pitton de Tournefort in his eighteenth-century work *Institutiones rei herbariae*—is a Sinhalese word, and it was the lotus, in all its configurations, from physical flower to religious offering, cultural artifact and political emblem, that had brought me to Sri Lanka. I'd flown thirteen hours from New York to Doha, Qatar, and another five from Doha to Colombo, this island country's modern capital. From there, we (myself and Nayomi Apsara, a forty-three-year-old filmmaker and poet, who was my guide and translator) had driven five hours and 124 miles to the ancient capital of Anuradhapura, located amid the lakes and jungles of the north, where we met Asoka before dawn. The lake, where he leases his section for less than $100 a month, was thirty minutes from the city. Nayomi and I were in a rented car; Asoka, in his white auto-rickshaw. We stopped to receive the blessings of a roadside Ganpati, the deity considered a remover of obstacles in both Buddhist Sri Lanka and Hindu India. In the half-light, bumping along a red-earth road, I saw that the land was full of water. We passed the hulking forms of whole trees half submerged in lakes, their canopies dark against the brightening sky. Cormorants and herons sunned themselves in the first rays of the morning. A rust-breasted jungle fowl strode along the edge of the water. We passed a sign that read DO NOT PICK THE FLOWERS, THE LAKE HAS BEEN LEASED FOR CULTIVATION. A column of blue smoke rose from the paddy fields. The cemented foundations of the village houses were stained brownish red, their freshly swept front yards enclosed by trees whose fruits and flowers—banana, hibiscus, papaya—are used in ritual prayers, or puja, as well as for ornamentation and consumption. Outside one such house, painted a bright orange, Asoka's landlords, an uncle and nephew in short-sleeved shirts and *saramas* (sarongs), greeted us. And then we followed the lotus farmer into the ooze.

"Growing in the mud, and yet so clean, the lotus is a symbol of purity" writes the Sri Lankan historian Ananda K. Coomaraswamy in his 1913 book, *The Arts and Crafts of India & Ceylon*. The lotus pool, he continues, "with leaves and flowers in bud, widely opened, and again dying down, is an image of the ebb and flow of human life (*samsara*)."

IT'S AMAZING WHAT a flower will tell you about a society, if you let it. In Sri Lanka, I wanted to follow the lotus out of the murk, where it was cultivated by men like Asoka, into shop stalls where enterprising sellers put it into the hands of devotees. I wanted to see it enter stone, transformed by the sculptor's chisel into an ornament as commonplace as the egg-and-dart motif in classical Western architecture. It was a journey that would take me from Sri Lanka's oldest capital at Anuradhapura, to its medieval seat of power, at Polonnaruwa (sixty-six miles south), then to Kandy (some eighty miles further south), the island kingdom's last royal capital, now a lakeside town of 1.5 million set among colonial-era tea plantations, rolling hills, and rainforest. In each of these places, the signifier of kingship had been the possession of a sacred relic, a tooth of the Buddha, which had been spirited away from India in the hair ornament of a princess in the fourth century and now resided at the Temple of the Tooth (Sri Dalada Maligawa) in Kandy. Buddhism itself had come to the island from India in the third century BC, and it was Theravada, "The Way of the Elders" in Pali, the language of Buddhist liturgy, that was practiced here, as in Myanmar, Cambodia, and Thailand.

In the lake, fish nibbling at my feet, Asoka showed me the tiny curled tip of the lotus leaf emerging from the water. "First the leaf comes out," he said. "One leaf, one bud, and the flower blossoms in the shade of the leaf. It protects it, like a parasol." He'd been here only the day before, in his dinghy, harvesting some 1,700 flowers, 400 stems at a time. These he sold to the sellers in the precincts of the Ruwanwelisaya stupa in Anuradhapura for 40 rupees (13 cents) a stem. They, in turn, sold them on to devotees for four or five times that amount.

Watching Asoka leaning down, measuring the calyx of one flower against the length of his forearm, showing me how to pluck its fibrous rough-napped stalk (never pull; it's a swift back-and-forth, like breaking a chicken neck), I was reminded that this gentle matinal scene was the site of sexual revelry the night before. The lotus flower, a great seductress who lives but three days, uses her subtle aquatic scent—which grows heavier by the hour through a process known as volatilization—to draw insects into her boudoir. As night falls, the petals close, trapping the hexapods within. "Encouraged by the warmth," writes the British horticulturist Mark Griffiths in *The Lotus Quest: In Search of the Sacred Flower* (2009), "the hostages feed and frolic on a litter of pollen shed by the golden anthers. The oubliette becomes the scene of an orgy." In the morning, the petals reopen, releasing the pollen-covered insects into the chill air. The shock of being so suddenly exposed makes them unable to tell morning from evening. So all around me now, drowsy six-legged sexual prisoners, in what Griffiths calls "a false dusk," were in search of comfort in newly opened lotus pads, different from those in which they had spent the night, thereby acting as unsuspecting agents of dissemination.

Asoka swiped open the petals of one calyx, like a man counting a wad of cash, and showed me its white-tipped anthers and tiny yellow receptacle. There are dozens of varieties of lotus, he explained, but "what we have in this lake is a special one," a variety known as *siapat*, or hundred-petaled. He then broke open a fully mature receptacle to reveal a green, bean-shaped seed. Inside, the white, mealy texture tasted like almond flesh. Ahead of me, standing in several inches of mud and water, Nayomi (whose surname, Apsara, means celestial nymph) was posing with a pink lotus in her hair.

"It's our flower, it's our treasure," Asoka said as we parted that morning, "and it's a lot of people's bread and butter. It only ever brings prosperity to a country," he added pointedly, "never disparity."

The lotus is indeed one of nature's miracle plants, whose uses from root to flower are myriad. The rhizome is eaten in soups and stir-fries all over south and east Asia. Griffiths calls it "a natural chemical factory," containing powerful antioxidants, oils, acids, alkaloids, and vitamins that are anti-inflammatory. It's used in Chinese and Ayurvedic medicine to treat stomach ailments in particular, but also fever and insomnia. The plant's fibers produce a beautiful sturdy fabric called lotus silk, while the hydrophobic genius of its leaves are studied in biomimicry to develop new kinds of paints and coatings with special anti-fouling properties.

Asoka took pride in the magical properties of the lotus, even as he gestured to what had been the worst economic crisis in the island country's modern history. Sri Lanka, or Ceylon as it was known then, was a British colony from 1802 until 1948. The British were the last in a series of maritime empires—the Cholas, the Portuguese, the Dutch—who made incursions on Sri Lanka's shores, testing the island nation's special genius, shared by places like Japan, for assimilation and absorption while fiercely remaining itself. After independence, the new country had dreams of using its strategic position at the crossroads of sea trade to become an economic power, like Singapore would go on to be, but, by 1983, it was plunged into a three-decade civil war that drove a wedge between its Sinhalese majority and Tamil minority and set the stage for the authoritarian rule of two brothers, Mahinda and Gotabaya Rajapaksa, peddling their brand of ethno-nationalist populism. They adopted the lotus calyx as the insignia for their Sri Lanka Podujana Peramuna, or People's Front. When I was last here, in 2013, the Rajapaksas were riding a wave of Sinhalese triumphalism, having brought the war to a brutal end. Gotabaya was defense minister at the time. A decade later, his tenure as president had decimated the country's economy. In 2022, after massive shortages of fuel and other essentials, a popular revolt called the *aragalaya*, meaning "struggle" in Sinhala, had broken out, leading to his ouster (Mahinda, who was reappointed prime minister by his brother two years before, resigned subsequently), but Sri Lanka, despite the efforts of a new government to get the country back on its feet with a bailout from the International Monetary Fund, was still suffering. In September 2024, in Sri Lanka's first election since the economic collapse two years earlier, the country elected left-of-center Anura Kumara Dissanayake its new president.

On the way up to Anuradhapura, I'd stopped to see Jagath Weerasinghe, one of Sri Lanka's most eminent art historians and archaeologists. Sitting in his studio outside Colombo among paddy fields edged with coconut trees, the moist morning heat already oppressive, I asked Weerasinghe why he thought the lotus in particular had emerged as the emblem and artifact of an entire culture, how it could be both a physical object, real and usable, profaned by commerce and exalted by prayer, as well as a motif that transcended its natural state. "That's a good question," said Weerasinghe, who was nearly seventy, with a dark beard and a balding head, before venturing, "the lotus, situated in mud and water, comes out of this dirty background to be extremely beautiful and pure. It opens with the sun. It's almost like the story of Genesis. The origin of life. It has all the attributes to accommodate our idea of purity, but purity cannot be without its opposite. There's a link between the two."

The lotus hasn't just been co-opted by political parties in Sri Lanka but across the Palk Strait, in India, too, where the flower in full bloom is the insignia of Prime Minister Narendra Modi's Hindu supremacist Bharatiya Janata Party, or BJP. Yet everyday devotees (including Weerasinghe) are able to compartmentalize the invariable debasement politics brings as they offer the sacred flower up to their gods. As with any icon that's so many things to so many people, every detail of its use is pregnant with semiotic power. I had grown up among a culture of flowers in India, bequeathed to me by the women in my life. My grandmother at dawn would have me collect the coral-stemmed *harsinghar* (*Nyctanthes arbor-tristis*), which had fallen on the ground overnight, and which she used in her morning prayers. My mother, if she'd been out to dinner, would bring home strings of jasmine from street sellers at traffic lights to lay in a silver tray at her bedside, their scent mixing with the delicious cold draft from the air conditioner. We used gladioli for funerals and official occasions; the smell of white-and-yellow *Nargis* (*Narcissus poeticus*) was inseparable to me from the onset of North Indian winter; I loathed the fat-faced orange marigolds, which were used in weddings and worship. In Varanasi, I had seen altars of flowers meticulously built in the sanctum sanctorum of temples and brought crashing down in a metaphor of impermanence.

Flowers are threaded through every aspect of our life in India, our festivals, our seasons, our manners, but nothing is incidental, careless, or devoid of meaning. In the United States, too, flowers take on the burden of our joys and sorrows. They act as conduits of thanks, honor, love, appreciation, or simply ornamentation, and there is code inscribed into pigment and type, such as the various colors of the rose and what they signify, yet, in India, that grammar feels stricter somehow. One might, for instance, greet someone with a garland of flowers but one would garland the picture only of someone who was dead. Within this highly mitigated language of flowers, the lotus is supreme. An idea, no less than a flower.

A few days before my arrival in Sri Lanka, my grandmother in whose house I first tasted oudh, and who would have me gather harsinghar for her prayers, had died without seeing me. My exile from India made it impossible for me to return for her funeral. My husband put his arms around me and offered to take me to an Indian restaurant on the Upper West Side that night to honor my poor departed *nani*. It was all that could be done, but it was too little. I had grown up in her house; she was the person closest to me after my mother; I felt utterly destitute at having no rite of closure more profound than dinner at a restaurant. I had lived with the absurdity of watching my father's death (and its aftermath) on television and social media; but I told myself that at least I was estranged from him. My grandmother was someone I loved, and who loved me; I wanted to stop all the clocks; I did not just want to have to get on with my day. The only consolation I had was that my mother, who had planned to come to Sri Lanka anyway to see me, was here now—and so what had been planned as a little fortuitous mother-son time, on the doorstep of the country I had grown up in, but could no longer return to, acquired the quiet solemnity of a rite of remembrance.

FLOWERS ARE ENDURING, yet mutable, symbols, upon which our collective imagination inscribes meaning. The peony signified prosperity in Tang China; violets stood for virtue in nineteenth-century Europe; the azalea represents feminine elegance and temperance in Japan. The West had a long, complicated relationship with florals, as well as with deeper, headier fragrances, seeing in the essence of flowers an expression of their own relationship to sex, sanitation, the Orient— ideas of ethnic and cultural purity as made visible against the screen of the Other. The transition of a natural entity, such as the rose, the acanthus, or the fleur-de-lis into a totem is essentially an authorless process, in which an entire enterprise of sculptors, artisans, bards, and poets, each working within tradition, expresses the cultural yearnings of a society. A naturally growing leaf, or flower, an obscure motif from an older civilization, is elevated and transformed into the recognizable mark of what a society wishes most to express about itself, be it purity, power, fertility, or regeneration. No single moment, or inflection point, defines this transformation; it's rather the work of generations in which tradition, acting as the reservoir of many individual talents—the supreme artist, as it were— corrals and collects, lovingly nurturing that will one day be the defining mark of a society or culture.

The lotus first appears in the subcontinent upon Indus Valley seals, circa 2600–1900 BC, predating both Buddhism and Vedic Hinduism. The German Indologist Heinrich Zimmer, writing in the 1940s, postulated that the flower personified a Mother Goddess, a sister of the Akkadian Ishtar, the Phoenician Astarte, and Egyptian Isis, who was herself a prototype of Lakshmi, the Hindu goddess of prosperity. With the arrival of the Aryans, around 1900 BC, Lakshmi was gradually unseated from her lotus pedestal, and other divinities from the Vedic pantheon, such as the demiurge, Brahma, seated in her stead. As Vedic Hinduism took root in India, the lotus seat became the mark of divinity itself, expressed in Hindu-Buddhist cosmology by the idea that the gods are those whose feet do not touch the earth. Prajñā-Pāramitā, the Buddhist goddess of enlightened wisdom, is personified as a lotus, while in the esoteric school of Tantric (or Trika) Buddhism, as widely practiced in Tibet, China, and Mongolia, the "heart-lotus" serves as a key iconographic aid for "inner visualization." In the fire ritual of the Shingon tradition of Japan, the altar-hearth is shaped like a lotus.

As a student of Sanskrit, the lingua franca of the elite in ancient India, I had encountered the flower as the source of endless tropes and metaphors, but, rereading one of my favorite plays—*Malati and Madhava* by the eighth-century dramatist Bhavabhuti—I lost count of the number of times it appears. There are "the dark lotuses" of the protagonist's eyes and "breasts pale as fresh-cut lotus stalks"; there's "the fragile lotus-thread of hope" and the "tormented beauty of her limbs, like a lotus beneath the strong caress of the sun." For me, as a cultural Hindu, no creation story is more powerful than that of lotus-naveled Vishnu, the god of preservation, asleep on a cosmic ocean after the dissolution of the world. He rests upon the Snake of Residue, with his wife and consort, Lakshmi, at his feet. Eons roll by, and the waters gradually heat with regenerative energy, or *tapas.* Then, like the rainbow in Genesis, signifying the promise of rebirth, a lotus calyx sprouts from Vishnu's navel. Its petals open to reveal Brahma, the creator, who sets about making the world anew.

Weerasinghe was naturally irreverent, but when he spoke of his love of visiting the sacred bodhi tree at Anuradhapura with a single white lotus, every trace of irony disappeared. "All of a sudden," he said, "this stupid Marxist becomes part of a huge history, a tradition, part of a larger community. I feel like I belong." He described the Rajapaksas' appropriation of the flower as sacrilegious: "They're exploiting our cultural identity."

LATER THAT AFTERNOON, the dull mesmeric drone of chanting in Pali pierced the permanent air of afternoon that hung over the Sanctuary at Tissawewa, an old colonial-era hotel, near the Ruwanwelisaya stupa, where Nayomi, my mother, and I were staying. It was a place of sloping red-tiled roofs and planters' chairs in open arcades of whitewashed pillars. There were peacocks in glossy-leaved Indian almond trees in the garden. The sapping heat was of a piece with the aura created around the stupa by the chanting. It didn't so much call you to prayer as it enveloped you in its atmosphere.

We drove a few miles to the stupa where hundreds of worshippers, in their austere white, were streaming toward that great reliquary mound. It was over twenty centuries old, though newly whitewashed, a giant Buddhist flag (blue, yellow, red, white, and orange) in satin wrapped about its waist like a belt. The sight of its immense stone hemisphere rising out of the surrounding jungle put one in mind of nineteenth-century scenes of archaeological discovery. The temple-goers, each bearing a cornucopia of flowers, approached the stupa by a causeway, lit a lamp in a glass gazebo on the left, then proceeded forward, made their offering of flowers, circled the shrine, and were subsumed in an air of chanting and contemplation. Each was a free-ranging particle, dancing about in quantum chaos, until brought into the orbit of the stupa, and each gave a picture of modern Sri Lanka. There was Damintha, a fifty-two-year-old sergeant major, who'd served in the Sri Lankan army from 1992 to 2012 and lost an eye in a grenade attack. He was there with his wife, bearing bowls of jasmine and pink lotus, grateful that the war was over and that the once-heavy security presence surrounding the stupa was gone. My mother had covered that war as a young reporter out of New Delhi. It was also here, in the early 1990s, not far from Anuradhapura, that she first lost her nerve as a reporter covering conflict. She was in her forties when she turned back from a war zone. "You get to an age when you just can't do it anymore," she said. Ahead we met Dematulawa Sugathasiri, the forty-year-old head monk of a nearby monastery. He stood among a troupe of younger monks in burgundy robes, ranging in age from twelve to twenty-one, carrying lilac switches of long-stemmed water hyacinths. "When Siddhartha attained nirvana," the monk explained, "he spent seven weeks meditating on different things, of which the sixth was the lotus. Siddhartha walked as soon as he was born"—the monk added—"and even though his mother stood under a different tree, it was lotuses that bloomed as he took his first seven steps."

Evening fell, and the floodlights came on. Dimithi Nimatha, a thirty-year-old woman who lived near the stupa, was engaged in the performance of an extraordinary offering. On a stone table, twenty-four pink lotuses were arranged in three rows on a bed of yellow petals, with twenty-four lamps on heart-shaped plates. The number was important: it represented the twenty-four conditions for the existence of reality as outlined by the Buddha, such as simultaneity, contiguity, association, and disassociation. As Nimatha spoke, I marveled at the unabashed intellectuality of Buddhism. It felt to me, in that moment, like the only truly adult religion, almost as if the works of Schopenhauer, or Kant, had been made the basis of a creed. Other faiths made concessions to the faithful; they reached people of all levels, sometimes in the form of crude but powerful concepts, such as heaven and hell, or then in the promise of an eternal soul. An economy of guilt and reward kept the believer in thrall. Buddhism, like certain writers who trust their readers, offered little beyond the austere and difficult teaching of the Buddha—a teaching that made no claims to divinity, or revelation, and did not need faith or devotion to be apprehended. What it required was discipline, self-observation, and—the reason I feel there's so little age on Buddhism—what we require today too: concentration. The Buddha had no need for God, but worship and ritual had found their way into his teaching. "When Buddhism declines," Nimatha said, peering at us out of bifocal glasses, "these conditions are lost, so we are performing this puja in order to sustain them."

Outside, the commerce of flowers was underway. Sameera and Sunetra, a brother-sister duo in their thirties, had quite literally cornered the market with their shop near the entrance to the stupa. Sameera had dark tattooed arms and a French beard and wore a tweed cap over his thick curly hair. "It's a good business," he said, flashing me a smile of crowded teeth, as he swiped open the petals of a lotus. When I asked him where his flowers came from, he said offhandedly, "everywhere," but in fact he meant a triangle of deep forest and lakes, stretching south from Anuradhapura to the ancient cave temples of Dambulla and the medieval capital of Polonnaruwa. The trade was informal, hardly even on the radar of the Ministry of Agriculture, which gave no subsidies to lotus farmers, but there was a distinct supply chain comprised of men like Asoka (one of Sameera and Sunetra's suppliers), like so many individual flowers held together by a submarine network of roots. On the outskirts of Anuradhapura, I met Indika Dilhani, a forty-two-year-old mother, who ran a lotus stall by the side of the highway. She worked from 5:30 a.m. to 9:00 p.m., earning as little as $6.50 on a good day, in order to provide for her son and husband who'd been paralyzed after a motorcycle accident in 2017.

"I have suffered in this life because of the sins of a previous life," she said, with the casual fatalism of those who believe in the transmigration of the soul—though *not* in its permanence, which the Buddha famously eschewed in his doctrine of *annata*, or non-self—"but I believe that selling lotuses, even if a business, will bring me good karma, and my next life will be better."

IF THERE'S ONE flower with which the lotus has historically been confused, in art and literature, as well as in science, it's the water lily (*Nymphaea*). It makes sense that the two aquatic flowers—the lotus is India's national flower while the water lily is Sri Lanka's—would seem like near cousins, but, interestingly, Griffiths tells us, modern DNA studies have shown that the lotus's "closest living relations" are not water lilies at all, or even other aquatic plants, but rather plane trees and Southern Hemisphere shrubs, such as banksia, embothrium, and protea. On my last visit to Sri Lanka, I had seen what I thought were lotuses in cave paintings in Sigiriya, a fifth-century rock fortress, where Weerasinghe is the director of archaeology, but he corrected me, then gave a fascinating reason why: they were *too* realistic. The lotus, once it had entered stone, would have been too invested with aesthetic meaning, too codified and stylized, to be depicted as realistically as the flowers in Sigiriya, which were mere flowers subject to the individual artist's fancy. Asian art, Weerasinghe explained, did not have what he called the "mimesis problem." "They did not want to create the world as it looked," he said. "If a statue of Venus were to come alive, we'd say, 'Come on, get dressed,'" Weerasinghe said, making a contrast with Greco-Roman art, "but if the [goddess] Tara [a fierce embodiment of the female principle, a Buddhist Kali] were to come alive, you'd run away." Weerasinghe advised that I go to Polonnaruwa instead, where I'd see firsthand how much room for innovation was permitted the traditional artist, working within the constraints of form and mindful of what had gone before (tradition in Sanskrit, or *parampara*, literally implies continuity), how much was too much.

The drive to Polonnaruwa took us through dense forest where wild elephants ambled along the side of the road, followed by flocks of butterflies at their feet. Everywhere was water, and wherever there was water, there were colonies of lotuses growing in the shallow parts. The heat had made entire towns retreat behind sharply delineated margins of shadow. Women carried parasols, and darkness lingered heavily beneath deep eaves. Mosquito nets in pastel colors hung from the corrugated roofs of shops, like toys over a cradle, and brightly lettered signs in Sinhalese, crammed into small rectangles, added to the garishness of the day.

The lotus was ubiquitous that afternoon in Polonnaruwa. It ran like connective tissue through the twelfth-century temple complex of age-blackened Buddhas, red earth, and large-leaved verdure, its ubiquity reminding me of how much I had encountered it in Sanskrit poetry. It appeared now as a decorative motif edging the semicircular moonstones outside temples whose facades had fallen away, now as a seal of sorts, stamped into the capital of a pillar. To have been so recently with the physical flower and to see it now, a feature of architecture, was to understand the process of paring down and simplification that made it possible for the essence of a living thing to be enshrined in stone.

At Polonnaruwa, one felt the creativity of the individual artist chafe against the strictures of form. As with a medieval bard composing a sonnet, the sculptor found ways to push the limits, threading a course between continuity and cliché. At first glance, an ordinary raised stone platform, known as the Nissankalata Mandapa, late twelfth century, was just another ruined temple, open to the sky, with a stupa at its center. Closer, one saw the playfulness that had inspired its columns, which were undulating lotus stalks, draped in tendrils, with full-blown flowers for capitals. At the *neelum pokuna*, or lotus pond, located some distance from the main complex down a desolate tree-lined road, the sculptors seemed to have taken a special meta pleasure in using the shape of the eight-petaled lotus, with eight sinking tiers, as a framing device for a pond that, though dry now, would once have been full of the sacred flowers.

It was evening when we arrived in Kandy, after a four-hour drive out of the forests and lakes of the north. The town's lights were visible through an opening in the hills, strewn over the darkening valley. In the morning, percussive drumming from the Temple of the Tooth resounded through the low forested hills. Kandy Lake was green, trimmed with flowering trees and a low crenelated wall, known as a cloud wall, pierced with small triangular alcoves for oil lamps.

The Temple of the Tooth is a vast complex on many floors, with many subsidiary shrines and a library of manuscripts. Once again we were greeted with an endless stream of

pilgrims in white. Outside, Nayomi informed me that worshippers pledged a specific number of lotuses related to a specific ask, but as I talked to them, the ask was heartbreakingly
the same: everyone wanted to get away from the blighted island. Anoma Nilangani, a fifty-four-year-old mother and the
wife of an English teacher, had made a vow five months ago
that if her job, as a housemaid in Bahrain, came through, she
would return to the temple and make an offering of fifty-four
white lotuses. She was with her fifteen-year-old son, giving
thanks to the Buddha for letting her escape Sri Lanka. There
was thirty-year-old Ishani, in a striking white sari, with nine
lotuses, expressing gratitude that her husband had found a
job as a restaurant manager in Malaysia. On my flight to Colombo, a few days earlier, I had sat next to Ushan, who worked
at a seat belt factory in Romania. In excruciating detail, he
walked me through a laundry list of all the things—a house,
a car, fuel—he would never be able to afford if he lived in Sri
Lanka. It was why he had taken a factory job, in a faraway
country, unable to communicate with the people around him.
Sri Lanka was hemorrhaging its young, educated workforce,
and, in a strange irony, it was the flower that the Rajapaksas
had chosen as their emblem that was now the messenger of
their ravages.

In Kandy, I stayed with Channa Daswatte, a mentee of
the great Sri Lankan architect Geoffrey Bawa and a friend,
who took me on a tour of lotuses in the lesser-known temples surrounding Kandy. "It's obscenely pervasive," Daswatte
said, pointing to the flower as a space filler, white lotuses on a
red ground, at the fourteenth-century Lankatilaka Viharaya

Temple, then at the keystone of what he described as "an arch of prosperity." Hindu gods lurked in the shadows, behind a golden Buddha, denoting an easy syncretism between the two religions. He held out a cloth mat in the shape of a lotus, which he conjectured would've become commonplace with the arrival of Singer sewing machines in the late nineteenth century—modern means by which people could express their ancient affection for the flower. Daswatte recalled that as chairperson of the Geoffrey Bawa Trust he had held an exhibition in 2019 marking Bawa's centenary and had commissioned work from Chandraguptha Thenuwara, one of Sri Lanka's best-known contemporary artists. Thenuwara used his commission to create a subversive two-faced lotus, into which he worked images from the authoritarian rule of the Rajapaksas—the dreaded white vans that disappeared the regime's critics, the war crimes, the brutal slum clearance described as beautification. As Daswatte spoke, I realized that the semiotic game of appropriating powerful symbols, like the lotus, and imbuing them with fresh meaning is never truly concluded—and, moreover, two can play at it, just as the stars-and-stripes can simultaneously be the preserve of a modern artist like Jasper Johns as well as the field to which the public imagination returns again and again, sometimes working a blue line into its stars and spangles in support of law enforcement, other times turning it red, black, and green in service of David Hammons's pan-African flag, or just hanging it upside down in a bipartisan gesture of protest. Thenuwara similarly had reclaimed the cherished Sri Lankan flower from the Rajapaksas, making it bear witness to their crimes. "It's the lotus," Daswatte said of the series Thenuwara had made, "but what is it hiding?"

In Colombo, the flower had also been the subject of an exhibition at the Museum of Modern and Contemporary Art Sri Lanka that had closed several months before I arrived. On my last day in the country, I sat with Sandev Handy, one of the museum's curators, at a coffee shop outside its entrance. Handy, in his early thirties, was all in black, with white sneakers and a thick black beard. The exhibition included a captivating painting of lotuses by the Sri Lankan artist Senaka Senanayake—a subject he returned to again and again in his work—as well as a larger work, showing flora and fauna, that had been commissioned for the fifth summit of the Non-Aligned Movement (a conference of newly independent and developing countries that sought neutrality in the Cold War), which was held in Colombo in 1976. Using a range of media (a literary magazine, a novel, a stamp), Handy walked me through the way the metaphor of the lotus had come to be laden with postcolonial significance. "Who's included in the mud, who's included in the lotus?" Handy asked rhetorically. Was this ancient symbol of regeneration rising out of the miring mud of colonial history? Handy was keen to point out that assertions of purity are rarely benign. In places like Sri Lanka and India, the rediscovery of a precolonial self had given way to the ethno-nationalism of which the lotus was once again the central focus. It was easy to blame demagogues of various stripes for exploiting our shared desire to live in a time unmolested by the outside gaze, but we were all guilty of trying to turn back the clock to a time before the rupture. My parents—one in India, the other in

Pakistan—had both lost language and been forced to relearn Hindi, Urdu, and Punjabi as adults. They wished to live in the continuities of an instinctive past, when the coming of the British had not occurred, even though that rupture, with all it contained—English, modernity, the Western gaze—was the single most important cultural event in their lives. The idea of return is false. The past is not to be papered over. The purity of the lotus does not exist at the exclusion of the impurities that are its lifeblood, but *because* of them, linked to them, as it were, by a vital cord.

Then Handy showed me a photograph by the contemporary artist Abdul Halik Azeez (who goes by Halik) of a girl with smiling eyes standing in the wreckage of her recently "beautified" community. She held a mirror in her hands, reflecting the 1,155-foot-high Lotus Tower in Colombo—a Rajapaksa-era construction. I'd seen it on my first day in the Sri Lankan capital. It had a garish green stem and a bulbous pink head, a self-serving landmark, all steel and glass, that dominated the Colombo skyline and vacuously changed color at night.

I spent my final hours in Colombo in Halik's uncarpeted house in the gentrifying suburb of Rajagiriya. The fluorescent-tube-lit room was full of books on feminism, neoliberalism, and art; a jackfruit tree outside was laden with its spike-covered bounty. In February 2018, when Halik had taken his iconic image in a neighborhood adjacent to the Lotus Tower that was in the process of being demolished, the Rajapaksas' hold on power could not have been more secure. "The Lotus Tower," Halik said, "is one of the primary symbols the state came up with to convince itself of the possibility of becoming a world-class city." Halik, having witnessed his country buried in debt, was full of a critique of the neoliberalist tendency to try to instill unrealistic aspirations in the populations of developing countries. Two years later, the Rajapaksas were gone, but the tower stood as a proof not just of their hubris, but of the kind of debt-laden populism that had brought the island nation to its knees, its ports ransomed out to the Chinese for decades to come. In analyzing the politicized lotus as a symbol in the Rajapaksa era, Halik said a lot depends on where and in what form it appears. In my lifetime, I had seen the once-beloved likeness of the monkey god Hanuman acquire a threatening militarized character when it began to appear in black-and-saffron on the backs of auto-rickshaws in Indian cities, heralding the arrival of the Modi era. Halik said the Sri Lankan lion had undergone a similar transformation, becoming synonymous with the ethno-nationalism of the Rajapaksas. The lotus, he felt, had been spared the same fate, even as Halik had seen his own image of Rajapaksa hubris acquire a different color in light of their downfall. "It travels," Halik said, in what was true of semiotics more generally, "and it acquires a kind of currency that's beyond your control."

In Colombo, I said goodbye to my mother. Throughout her time in Sri Lanka, she had been receiving messages from Modi's office. The prime minister wanted to send her a letter of condolence on the passing of my grandmother, oblivious to the distress he had caused my nani by preventing her from seeing her grandson in her last days. My mother had been stonewalled by the Prime Minister's Office for the past five years, as she had tried to plead my case. Now they were in touch. She used the opportunity to write to Modi to tell him how my grandmother had brought me to India for the first time as a two-year-old on her back; I had grown up there; I should be allowed to return to visit my family. My mother's entreaties were met with silence. It was cruel. What she had mistaken for a thaw was merely the sadistic munificence of the strongman. She was seventy-four and, with every parting now, I felt her frailty. I feared that if my situation with regard to India did not change, then one day I would receive a phone call telling me that she, too, had gone, and that was more absurdity than I was equipped to deal with.

I left the island before dawn. Dark bodies of water lay beneath me at whose edge grew the sacred flower. Now, at 4:00 a.m., a time of inner contemplation known as "the hour of Brahma," I imagined the first touch of morning spreading over the tear-shaped island. In my mind's eye, I saw thousands of lotus buds opening, releasing groggy pollen-covered insects into the cold air of a new day. How wild it was that we, human beings, had inserted ourselves into these daily rituals. What is the culture of flowers if not the human imagination, full of whimsy and ingenuity, insinuating itself into the lives of these vegetal entities? The lotus especially was the supreme flight of fancy. In the everyday routine of this aquatic flower, an entire culture had found spiritual expression. In the opening and closing of its petals at first and last light, we had seen intimations of our own mortality—samsara, the cycle of creation and decay—and, in the sight of it resplendent over a bed of nourishing mud, we had recognized our longing to rise above the muck of our lives.

Pilgrimages

Bolivia, Mongolia, Iraq

Bolivia

IN LA PAZ, BOLIVIA, ONE AFTERNOON AT THE BEGIN-
ning of the year, I sat in an aerie of an apartment overlooking
an Andean amphitheater of bare scarified mountains. I was in
the home of Eduardo Quintela Gonzáles, a forty-year-old mu-
sicologist, as he told me how his late father would take him on
pilgrimages to the Basilica of Our Lady of Copacabana. They
would walk for three days from their home in La Paz, the
Bolivian seat of government, to the pilgrim town of Copacabana, at the edge of Lake Titicaca, ninety-five miles to the
northwest. "Walking alone at night changes one's perspective
of things," Quintela said. "When you set out, you think you're
going to talk to the people you're with. But after the first day,
you find you have nothing to say. It's just you and your will to
reach your destination."

The idea of a sacred destination, reached through penance and hardship, that reconfigures one's view of reality, is a feature of pilgrimage everywhere, but Quintela's return to Copacabana later that week for the Feast of the Virgin on February 2 was underpinned by a special sorrow: his father, the man who had made the trip to Copacabana fifteen times in his life, had died the year before after a bout of COVID-19, which was followed by a diagnosis of brain cancer, an operation, and then six months in a coma. "I prayed to the Virgin because he asked me to, but he died anyway," said Quintela, who was dressed in a black hoodie and jeans, as we sat on folding chairs in a room hung with stringed instruments and masks. I was headed to Copacabana, too. Quintela and his band were due to play at Mass on the morning of fiesta. It would be his first trip back since his father had died, and he was intent on honoring him at the site of his deepest devotion.

I was on a pilgrimage of sorts myself. From my home in New York, Bolivia would be my first stop in what I had envisaged as three journeys across three great faiths, spread out over a year: fiesta high in the Andes, where pre-Hispanic ritual and belief underlay Catholicism; a spring of pilgrimage through Buddhist and shamanic Mongolia; and lastly, a time of mourning in Shiite Iraq.

I was interested in pilgrimage as a kind of ur-travel, crucial to so much that we associate with the modern industry of tourism, from early inns, hostels, and brothels to guidebooks and travel writing. In their 1978 book, *Image and Pilgrimage in Christian Culture*, the British and British American anthropologists Victor and Edith Turner imagine pilgrimage as two roads, one inbound and one outbound—one sacred, the other profane. The road in is a spiritual journey, "exteriorized mysticism," to use the Turners' phrase. The road out is less about faith and more about travel itself—that radical business of leaving the safety of one's home to journey, as Chaucer writes in *The Canterbury Tales* (1400), "to ferne halwes, couthe in sondry londes" ("to far-off shrines, known in sundry lands"). The word *pilgrim* itself derives from the Latin *peregrinus*, meaning "one from abroad"—a foreigner. In India, where I grew up, and where the sacred topography of pilgrimage stitches the land together, the Hindi word for traveler, *yatri*, is still the same as the word for pilgrim. I remember afternoon naps with my grandmother in Delhi on days of savage heat, when she would exhort me to take her to the various holy sites, now the shrine of Vaishno Devi in the Himalayas, now the temple town of Varanasi, curled languidly about the Ganges. As in medieval Europe, pilgrimage, not tourism, was the primary motivation to travel at all for someone like my grandmother; years later, I was amazed to find that it was the same for my husband's grandmother, an evangelical Christian living in the American South. The first time Lyra Skinner, at eighty-five, got on a plane and left the Deep South was to go to the Holy Land. Pilgrimage made familiar the unfamiliar, allowing those who might not be persuaded to go to the nearest big city to venture thousands of miles away. Standing in the garden of Gethsemane, Lyra was struck most by how at home she felt.

In my twenties, I set out on my own pilgrimage, to Mecca, among other places, in search of the country and faith of my

Pakistani father, who was a stranger to me for most of my life. At the time, I had felt my own lack of religious belief as a severe limitation. I was too young then to see that faith, though a crucial ingredient in pilgrimage, was not all. "A cocktail of motives"—to borrow a term from the British writer Victoria Preston's 2020 book, *We Are Pilgrims: Journeys in Search of Ourselves*—sets us on the road to pilgrimage. In medieval times, one might be sent on a pilgrimage by a magistrate as a sentence for a crime. The Prophet Muhammad, having conquered all of Arabia in 630, clearing Mecca of its pagan idols in the process, went back two years later on a triumphant pilgrimage. The Crusaders saw themselves above all as pilgrims. Long before Quintela, the grief pilgrim had walked Jerusalem's Via Dolorosa, merging private anguish with the suffering of Christ.

I was interested in this other human side of pilgrimage—the road out, as it were. I imagined it to be full of danger and fun, populated with bawdy characters such as Chaucer's Wife of Bath. I had chosen three faiths that were at odd angles to my own background—my father was Muslim, but not Shiite; my paternal grandmother was Christian, but not Catholic; my mother was Sikh, which made her part of the Indic fold, but not Buddhist. A few months before I began my three pilgrimages, I found myself stricken with a loss of my own. Zinc, our beloved shepherd/Lab mix, became gravely ill and died soon after. For so many of us, pets become our whole lives. "Grief has its own exigencies," writes V. S. Naipaul in an essay about the death of his father, his younger brother, and his cat, Augustus. "We can never tell beforehand for whom we will feel grief." My husband, Ryan, and I had both known the oblique grief of trying to mourn fathers from whom we were estranged—both of whom were killed at gunpoint—but the sorrow we felt over Zinc was as direct a thing as we had ever known. On that first morning in La Paz, sitting in that garret of an apartment in Vino Tinto, a working-class neighborhood of winding treeless streets, listening to Quintela speak of his year of loss, I felt myself overcome with emotion—whether from the rawness of Zinc's death, the altitude, or the ghost of my unmourned father.

I WAS TO leave the city the next day at dawn with my guide, Monica Machicao. The plan was to drive deeper into the Altiplano, which is a world unto itself, a vast expanse of tableland spread across Bolivia, Chile, and Peru. We were headed to the edge of Lake Titicaca, about two hours away. The entire basin of the holy lake had been a site of pilgrimage long before the Spanish conquest, indeed long before the Incas themselves. On the way to Copacabana for fiesta, I wanted to make a brief stop at the romantically named Islands of the Moon and the Sun. They sit across the bay from the sanctuary of the Virgin of Copacabana and played a central role in the creation stories of this enclosed alpine culture.

At over twelve thousand feet, the air was as thin as glass. Nicholas Casey, the former Andes bureau chief for *The New York Times*, had warned me about the effects of the elevation. He advised that I start taking medicine to ward off altitude sickness while I was still in New York, but, despite the pills, I couldn't believe what the air in the Altiplano did to my body: the searing shortness of breath, the piston beating of my heart, the throbbing headache.

"We have millions more red blood cells than other people," Monica said, "plus our lungs are bigger." It was Casey who had introduced me to Monica, a veteran journalist in her fifties. In learning of her antipathy for the nativist politics of the former Bolivian president Evo Morales—the country's first Indigenous president, the man under whom the nation had been refounded in 2009 as the Plurinational State of Bolivia—I was given a foretaste of the inner tensions of the society I found myself in.

I grew up in postcolonial India, sloughing off two (or ten, depending on whom you ask) centuries of foreign rule, both British and Muslim. In one sense, the history of Bolivia resembles that of India. Both countries were subjugated by a European colonial power: Britain started conquering India two centuries after Spain's conquest of the Americas. Bolivia attained its independence from Spain in 1825, 122 years before India pushed out the British. In both countries, the preconquest society is in many ways intact. In Bolivia, whole nations of pre-Columbian peoples, such as the Aymara and the Quechua, have lived on, under varying layers of Hispanization, which has seeped through into every aspect of identity, from religion and culture to language and race.

If India was like Bolivia in one respect, it was like medieval Spain in another: both countries had known centuries of Muslim rule until, in 1492—the year that Columbus sailed to the Americas—a resurgent Catholic Spain expelled its last Muslim emir, completing what came to be called La Reconquista. It was that New World power that, under men like Hernán Cortés and Francisco Pizarro, would go on to conquer Aztec Mexico in 1521 and Inca Peru and Bolivia in the 1530s.

On that first day with Monica, listening to her speak of feeling like a racial outsider in a country where her ancestors had been for five centuries, I began to understand how fresh the wounds of this history still were. "What do they see when they see you?" I asked. "A white woman," she said. "And it's not true! My father's mother had Indigenous origins."

Leaving La Paz, past shanties, glitzy *cholets* (party halls), and shops full of televisions and washing machines, I soon set eyes on the Cordillera Real (the Royal Mountain Range) for the first time. The city was behind us, and we were in a vast grassland speckled with tiny habitations when, hovering to our right, there appeared the black and jagged shapes of high Andean peaks, their hollows filled with waxy disks of sunlit snow. Monica had spoken earlier of the holiness of mountains in Andean culture. One famous image of La Virgen del Cerro, the Virgin of the Hill, depicts her whole figure, save her hands, consumed by the mountain. "They are the true Hindus," a friend of mine with a long experience of South America messaged me, referring to the hybridity he had witnessed in the Altiplano. "They absorb everything and remain themselves."

Gazing at these holy eminences, their bases shrouded in mist, the summits piercing a band of clear blue sky above, I was intimately aware that this was part of the staggering spectacle of nature that had first inspired worship among the people of the Altiplano. Then, shortly after, the lake itself appeared. On that day of many moods, Lake Titicaca's pellucid waters were shades of silver, slate, blue, and charcoal and edged with reeds. It is an inland sea the size of Puerto Rico and, at 12,500 feet, the highest navigable lake in the world. A red-bottomed hydrofoil awaited at the small town of Huatajata, ready to take us deeper into what our guide on the boat described as the "sacred lake for our Andean civilization, the Andean Mecca."

On that bright January morning, the hydrofoil slipped through a narrow strait and the full immensity of the 3,200-square-mile lake—nearly half of which is in Bolivia, the rest in Peru—came into view. An hour or so later, the Islands of the Sun and the Moon appeared. They had low-crested hills, with Inca terraces, that rose out of the leaden water. On their summits I saw wheeling flights of mountain caracaras, coral-faced birds of prey. It was here that the pre-Inca deity Viracocha was said to have ordered the heavenly bodies to rise for the first time. On the Island of the Sun, I had wanted to hike the five or six miles to see the rock from which it's said that the sun had first risen, since this older site of pilgrimage was an antecedent of the Christianized fiesta, but, within hours of arriving, we were informed that it was unsafe to go to the sacred crag on foot. A conflict had broken out between two local communities, and the only way to reach the northern tip of the island was by boat. Our informant was Pablo Quisbert, an Indigenous researcher who had come over from Copacabana to join us for the day.

The lunch group Monica had assembled had all the makings

of a three-men-walk-into-a-bar joke. In addition to Quisbert, there was the Reverend Leandro Chitarroni, an Argentine priest whose numerous Bolivian parishioners influenced his decision to return to Copacabana for the Feast of the Virgin. There was also Andrés Eichmann Oehrli, a professor of Latin American literature at the Universidad Mayor de San Andrés in La Paz. Over peanut soup and steak with fries, I asked Father Chitarroni about the Roman Catholic Church's appropriation of Andean sanctity. "The problem we have all over the Americas," he said, "is when you give people the Good News and it is contrary to their local beliefs. We can introduce new things," he added, "but we have to let people keep their roots—the thoughts of their parents."

I was intrigued by Father Chitarroni's open embrace of syncretism. The Spain that conquered the New World, full of the religious zeal of La Reconquista (and the Inquisition), had been uniquely incapable of understanding how among the earth religions, like that of the Incas, it was possible to adopt new deities without forgoing the old gods. In *Conquistadores: A New History of Spanish Discovery and Conquest* (2021), the Mexican historian Fernando Cervantes writes that the arrival of every new bishop in the New World instigated a campaign aimed at the "extirpation" of "idolatry" in the Americas.

THAT AFTERNOON, WE all took a boat with a smoky outboard motor to the tip of the island. At sunset, we walked a short distance uphill to the sacred rock, which the conquistadors had stripped of its gold and silver sheeting. In his 1653 book, *Inca*

Religion and Customs, the Jesuit priest Bernabé Cobo writes that the reddish-green rock that we were now in front of, its vertical face some eighteen feet high, had been a gathering place for large groups of pilgrims who had come from far away. "Thus this place became so famous that its memory will live on among the Indians as long as they last," he writes.

No pilgrim now came to the spot where the sun had first risen, even though we all felt its strange Ozymandian power. What looked like a sacrificial table of white sandstone, surrounded by andesite blocks, prompted Quisbert to speak of *capacocha*, an Inca ritual in which children of both sexes were selected for sacrifice. The table was the object of tourist lore, scarcely a few decades old. Just as Catholicism had appropriated Andean sanctity, so now did tourism titillate visitors in a place where pilgrims had come with holy dread in their hearts.

Across the bay, a ghostly white basilica was preparing for its biannual fiesta, which would take place over two days and include several nights of revelry. Copacabana had been home to a pre-Christian shrine featuring what a Spanish chronicler had called a blue-stone idol, which was possibly female and fish-bodied. It had been part of this ancient nexus of pilgrimage that had included the Islands of the Sun and the Moon, but, in the sixteenth century with the arrival of the Spanish, its old sanctity had been reconsecrated in the figure of the Virgin. Standing between these two poles of pilgrimage, one defunct, one active, I couldn't help but wonder who the ultimate victors are in a land where conquest has brought about a rupture with the past, yet where the old culture has so thoroughly assimilated the new as to leave it unrecognizable.

This idea is embodied in the statue of the Virgin of Copacabana that the Indigenous artist Francisco Tito Yupanqui sculpted in the mid-1570s. The Spanish had been on the Altiplano for less than fifty years when the native sculptor, born in Copacabana, began depicting Mary in ways that subverted unspoken aesthetic norms of her as white and European. On seeing Yupanqui's early efforts, the Spanish bishop was brutal in his contempt, telling the artist that his depictions of Mary looked like a bearded man and that he was better suited to paint *la mona con su mico* ("a monkey with her baby"). But Yupanqui persevered, said Father Chitarroni: "His religious search had to fulfill a European aesthetic, but the image he did is mestizo." Sacred objects are often authorless. They are wholly created by the collective imagination of men and women, such as Venus rolling in from the sea in rock form at Cyprus, or the primordial *linga* or phallus becoming representative of Shiva. What makes the Yupanqui story so extraordinary is that it locates the individual artist behind the creation of a sacred object in a highly detailed narrative that scrambles the motives of art and religion.

Arriving in Copacabana the next morning by boat, I wandered through streets of red cinder block and brightly colored corrugated metal, all coalescing around the hulking mass of the basilica, which, with its tiled domes of greenish brown, dwarfed the pilgrim town of about ten thousand. Inside, at the center of a baroque altarpiece, was Yupanqui's Virgin, bathed in white fluorescent light. Rarely had I seen so arrestingly beautiful a rendering of Mary, dark and solemn-eyed. "The singularity of this Virgin," said Quisbert as we peered at her through the gloom of the basilica, "is not merely that an Indigenous artist created her—she's also an Indigenous Virgin. Not white, not Black, but *morena*." A beautiful word, to which the English *brown* does little justice.

Wandering the bowels of that vast church preparing for fiesta, we encountered the head priest, Friar Abelino Yeguaori, in his cocoa-colored Franciscan habit. He stood in a room that contained the Virgin's many dazzling outfits—with pinks, lilacs, blues, and reds and embroidered gold. They had been donated by devotees and included one in a plain forest green, with an insignia of two crossed rifles under a condor, for she is the patron saint of the police, too.

Friar Yeguaori was to lead the procession the next day but was full of worries. The weather was changeable, now rain, clouds, and mist; now bursts of bright mountain sunshine. The border with Peru, a major source of pilgrims, had been closed because of postelection turmoil there. He feared there would be scarcely one or two thousand pilgrims, instead of the usual thirty to forty thousand, which would be bad not just for morale but because fewer pilgrims meant a sizable loss in donations. Nor did it help that evangelism was on the rise all over South America. "They tell them they cannot adore images," Friar Yeguaori said, his brows beetling. "First they tell them God will punish them, then they take their money, saying, 'If you give us money, God will give you more.'"

BY MORNING, A sharp alpine sun had banished Friar Yeguaori's fears of a poorly attended feast. Black smoke from firecrackers drifted across the blue sky, and the calm of the square outside the church was broken by the mournful martial thud of drums and the asthmatic hiss of trombones. A full brass band, in gray suits and sunglasses—the Real Andinos (or Royal Andeans)—was preparing to welcome the first pilgrims to the Feast of the Virgin of Copacabana. A stream of beribboned SUVs stood outside the church awaiting blessings. In front of them were offerings of sparkling wine and, on paper plates, petals, red-capped bottles containing a dark viscous brew of alcohol and coca leaves, and clear plastic pouches of rice, sugar, and cinnamon. "My father used to bring me here," said Irene, a sixty-five-year-old fruit and vegetable seller in a blue polka-dot dress. She had come from La Paz with her daughter, Juana, and their white terrier, Blanquita. "In those days we came in trucks. There were no buses, and the road was just sand. He would tell me to get down on my knees and ask the Virgin for favor, and we would encircle the church just like that."

Irene's face shone with piety but, like the hajji, whose pilgrimage to Mecca gives him immeasurable esteem in his community, there was also an element of self-satisfaction. Pilgrimage cloaked itself in godliness and sacrifice, but its motivations were not always altruistic. In Varanasi, at a house of death where old people came to breathe their last—for to die in the holy city was to be free of the cycle of life and death—I had witnessed firsthand the sacrifices of children who left busy modern lives to fulfill the spiritual ambitions of their parents. Naipaul, in *India: A Wounded Civilization* (1977), describes the Hindu quietism of a fictional character in a well-known Indian novel as "parasitic: It depends on the continuing activity of others, the trains running, the presses printing, the rupees arriving from somewhere. It needs the world, but it surrenders the organization of the world to others." I wondered now if pilgrimage did not have something of that same quality, self-indulgence sublimated into piety.

Two kids came cartwheeling up to us in costume. There was an eight-year-old boy with a green-and-yellow mask and red coat dressed as a *kusillo*, a little devil, or trickster. His eleven-year-old sister was a milkmaid. They were performing a rustic dance called the Waka Waka. Their mother, Aracely Alcón, in white tights and pale orange eye shadow, was there, too. When Santiago, the boy, was four, Alcón told us, he fell from the second floor of a building and hit his head. "We thought he was dead," she said. He was paralyzed and could move only his head. "Our family are true believers of the Virgin, and I prayed, 'It's my son, don't take him away.' The Virgin is a mother, too. She understood my pain." A week later, the paralysis broke and, after a year of rehab, Santiago was back on his feet. "He's a walking miracle," Alcón said. "We come here dancing to thank the Virgin."

Father Chitarroni was dancing, too. He came up to us in a rented brown poncho carrying a staff. He was to play the key role of the *jilakata* (village leader) in the dance that was to ensue. "For these people, dance is like an offering, a prayer," he said. All around us festivity was erupting. It was noon and there were dozens of people in the forecourt of the church, with dozens more pouring in from the main square and surrounding streets beyond. A line of milkmaids in hoop skirts of bright green and orange came trundling into the church. The clamor of numerous brass bands filled the air. Old Aymara women in multilayered *polleras* (frilled skirts) in maroons and oranges, with aprons and bowler hats, appeared on the sloping street that led from the church to the sacred lake. Armed with bags full of petals, trumpet flowers, and leaves, they moved swiftly down the axial street ornamenting it, here with the Inca sun, there with the sign of the cross.

The westering sun burned away every trace of a morning drizzle. I was heading down the main street looking for Monica, when suddenly, resplendent in the daylight and framed against the mountains, there appeared a replica of Yupanqui's Virgin, dressed in white and gold. She was on a palanquin carried on the shoulders of six men. Behind her came an impressive formation of church and municipal leaders with satin sashes across their breasts. Friar Yeguaori was there, too, again in his Franciscan habit. Behind them were women in brown vicuña mantas and bowlers. The townspeople threw flowers at the procession as it went by, up to the gate of the sanctuary, where the Virgin was enthroned at the entrance. The local leaders sat on a podium facing her. "Today we celebrate the arrival of the Virgin of Copacabana, who came here in 1583 from Potosí and was made by the hands of Tito Yupanqui," began Copacabana's council president, who wore a blue-and-white sash.

The area outside the church had become a great stage. Troupe after stupendous troupe, consisting of musicians and dancers from all over Bolivia and as far afield as Argentina, made their way up the street performing for the Virgin.

Among the most striking dances was the Morenada, which some believe emerged from the plight of Black slaves in the silver mines of Potosí. The dancers wore white metal masks, green-and-white feathers, and hoop skirts with tassels. After sharing capfuls of Scotch, they began their dark dithyrambic dance, rattling the *matraca*, an instrument that Monica said imitates the clanking and heavy tread of slave chains. It felt like a protest dance, percussive and hypnotic, unashamed in its embrace of the signifiers of enslavement.

The most beautiful of the acts was by Uma Marka, a troupe whose name means "land of water." At the center was a man who played an Andean trumpet of war called a *pututu*. "I came from afar to fulfill my promise / because I love you with my soul," the man sang. "I will always cherish you, my beautiful little *morenita*. / I will always adore you, Copaca-beñita." Then, almost in the same breath, he began to sing in praise of Pachamama (Mother Earth), "shin[ing] in the cosmos." He was a schoolteacher from Warisata, one of the lake towns. When I asked him how it was so easy for him to sing to both the Virgin and Pachamama, he said, "Both of them are the same for us. The Virgin is the mother of God. Pachamama is the mother of the earth."

As the formal acts began to wrap up around 7:00 p.m., the spirit of fiesta started to spread through the confetti-strewn streets of the town. The members of Uma Marka passed around handles of Scotch. Half-consumed cans of beer lay at their feet. I was chewing a mouthful of coca leaves from a green plastic bag, and they gave the afternoon a wonderful, thrilling edge. There is always an underlying darkness to carnival, the creeping strangeness of masks and extreme drunkenness. As night fell, this mood, tinged with hints of dislocation and panic, took hold. Young men with haggard faces and gaping mouths roamed the streets. A featureless pounding music, emanating from an indoor arena, drifted up to my hotel room until well after 3:00 a.m.

I had spoken that evening to Amaru Fiorilo Barrios, the twenty-nine-year-old half-Dutch, half-Bolivian son of the owners of the Hotel La Cúpula, where we were staying. Dressed in a pink hoodie and turquoise cap, his long hair windblown, he told me of the powerful epiphany he'd had during the pandemic related to pilgrimage. Even as the tourist industry vanished from the face of the earth, "we were full all the weekends with pilgrims," Fiorilo said. The border with Peru had been closed, as it was now, but they came by foot. The Altiplano, said Fiorilo, goes beyond borders. It was an important point: pilgrimages are located within national boundaries even as they transcend them. The shrine of Santiago de Compostela is in Spain, but the pilgrimage does not belong to Spain any more than the pilgrimage to Mecca belongs to the Kingdom of Saudi Arabia, or the sacred landscape of the Buddha's life to the modern states of India and Nepal. Nations, of course, try to draw validity from being home to major pilgrimage sites, but the nineteenth-century nation-state, a jealous and petty master, can never quite attain the subtle complex of belief and belonging that pilgrimage engenders. Fiorilo, who'd grown up in a westernized atmosphere in La Paz, was conscious of the need to honor the old religion of the Altiplano. "It's very important to keep it"—that is, to adhere to it, he said—"because it's the identity of the people."

Pilgrimage is bigger than the nation and, though it derives its authority from religion, it's often bigger than religion, too. Like the journey to Mecca, which started as a pre-Islamic pilgrimage common to many tribes of the Arabian Peninsula, this fiesta is at bottom an emanation of Andean culture. The religious component acts almost as a framing device for the expression of distinctive cultural elements, rituals, customs, song, and dance, such as the Waka Waka or the ancient pre-Christian use of llama parts in sacrifice.

ON THE WAY to Mass the next morning, we passed young men still in their suits eating *fricase*, a pork stew of potatoes and hominy, from plastic containers. "Hangover food," Monica said. The church was full when we arrived. The air smelled of lilies. Worshippers streamed in and out with replicas of the Virgin in plastic cases stuffed with fake US dollars. In an altar to one side, Eduardo Quintela's band, Ensamble Sincrético (Syncretic Ensemble), was warming up. It gave me a pang to see him, still in his black hoodie, surrounded by a padre-violinist in a Franciscan habit and female vocalists with shawls about their shoulders. Watching Quintela, his face drawn inward in concentration, I felt all the power of his tribute to his father, who had first brought him on pilgrimage to Copacabana.

This was the road into the shrine, the spiritual journey, in which pilgrims came before the Virgin bearing grief, joy, and gratitude in their hearts. Her cult was fed by this stream of humanity, each confiding in her, and she, in turn, edified the private circumstances of each individual life through her munificence, making the one feel part of a whole. For her, of seemingly limitless patience, no human drama was too insignificant, too tawdry, too wretched or alien. Her maternal consolations rested on her acceptance, her love, her understanding. "What is secret in the Christian pilgrimage, then, is the inward movement of the heart," write the Turners.

As Mass got going, Ensamble Sincrético filled the gold-and-blue vault of the church with haunting music. "A Vuestros Pies Madre" ("At Your Feet, Mother"), they played. It evoked the spirit of an older Europe, even as it sounded unmistakably Indigenous—so much so that the Europeans who came after the original missionaries didn't recognize it as their own until they were shown the sheets on which it had been carefully scored. It was Christian missionaries—that endless flow of Jesuit, Augustinian, Dominican, and Franciscan friars—who primarily brought baroque music to Bolivia. It formed a deep synthesis here with a culture for which music was already a form of worship. As Quintela explained to me, referring to the Guarayos, an Indigenous group in northeastern Bolivia: "When they die, they must pass several tests [in order to reach the afterlife. One of them] is to cross a river on the back of an alligator who only advances to music. If he [the deceased] is not a good musician, the alligator devours the soul of the Guarayo."

Altar boys, swinging silver thuribles, came down the nave of the church, incense smoke wafting up behind them. Then came members of the clergy, some of whom, including Father

Chitarroni and Friar Yeguaori, I now knew, but who had been utterly transformed by pomp and circumstance. The bishop of El Alto led the Mass, and dignitaries, such as Senator Rodrigo Paz Pereira, whose father had been a president of Bolivia, were part of the congregation.

As Mass ended, we filed out behind the Virgin. The senator, dressed down in a brown jacket and jeans, said that Yupanqui's Virgin had a special importance against the background of postcolonial history. "She's a unifying figure, as well as their protectress," he said. "Through her, they can talk, they can communicate."

Outside, the streets were thronged with brass bands. One of the *prestes*—a key official in the organization of the pilgrimage—was bedecked in garlands of spring flowers like a fertility god. In the main square, Friar Yeguaori was leading the Virgin in a procession, stopping at every corner to ask for a special blessing—for the children, the town, the leadership, the country. I had wanted to find more examples of how the old pre-Columbian religion of the Altiplano merged with Catholicism. That afternoon I got my chance. Climbing Calvary Hill, where stations of the cross were installed in the 1950s, I could see the bay and town, rain-washed red against dark hills. At its summit, amid tombs and sleeping dogs, women sold models illustrating another key ingredient of pilgrimage: want, hard material want. There were plastic replicas of every conceivable kind of habitation, from empty plots of land to little green-roofed houses and condos; toy models of every brand and style of car, from SUVs to racy two-doors, and crude piles of fake American dollars and euros. Monica, with a son in college and a daughter who was about to start her master's degree program, bought two folders of academic degrees to be blessed by the Virgin. It was oddly moving to have this concrete insight into people's lives through the things they wanted most.

Descending Calvary, we came across a young couple standing in front of a statuette of the Virgin and a bright red model car. The woman was weeping, wiping away strands of long black hair from her face. An older man was performing a ritual of sorts with a little brass bell, burning coals and incense. Another, in a red bolero, stood at his side. Everyone seemed very drunk. Cups of beer were being passed around, some sipped, some deliberately spilled in honor of Pachamama.

When the ritual was done, we approached. They were Argentines of Bolivian origin who lived in Buenos Aires. They had come by car, driving for three days, bringing with them their own statuette of the Virgin. It seemed like a long way to come, but "if you love the Virgin, it doesn't matter how long the road is," they said. When I asked them about the rite, which would hardly have been out of place on the banks of the Ganges in Varanasi, the younger man, Axel, explained that it was a blessing. The man performing it was an amauta, a shamanic figure. The young couple desperately wanted a car of their own. "Whatever we desire, the Virgin will give us the power and the will," said Axel. Pilgrimage, though couched in spiritual aims, often bordered on sheer cupidity. Some wanted peace, love, and health, others an automobile, but everyone wanted something. When I asked Axel why his wife had been crying earlier, he said, "We need to have faith, and there's a lot of emotion [involved]." But was there no conflict between these two systems of belief, the Virgin and the amauta? "It's just a belief," the man in the red bolero said, casually expressing a great truth about the unthinking quality of its hold over us. "We believe in the priest, and we believe in the amauta."

The wizened-faced amauta sang. He rang his bell. He used incense, a holdover from the classical world everywhere, to entreat the Virgin to give the couple what they wanted. When he was finished, I asked him what his religion was. "Católico," the amauta said. But what about this rite? That was surely not Catholic. "It's from our ancestors," he said. "This was from before we were Catholic."

The fiesta ended as all good parties should: in shame, debauchery, ignominy, and tears. All around the main square, open-air stages had been erected. Boy bands in sequined jackets were dancing and playing. Men with their arms draped about one another's shoulders reeled through the streets. In a gold-pillared room with neon orange beams, one couple—she in red lace, he in a burgundy suit—had fallen asleep in each other's arms. A visibly drunk young man in a gray suit with a red tie strode up to me. He had seen me that morning at Mass taking notes. Turning to a toy representation of the Virgin, he said, "This is our culture, these are our values, this is our tradition. Everything we have, we owe to her." Then he implored me to drink and spill. "You have to ask," he said, looking at the doll with fresh urgency. "Whatever you want, she will give to you." I was not above asking. I had come out of a year of illness and malaise, in which my grief over Zinc had gotten tied up with my fears about a new novel. My longtime publisher had sat on it for months before passing. I was midcareer. I was afraid of being put out of business. In writing, as in life, we fetishize the beginning, all that youth and ambition. We love the idea of peace or resignation at the end, in our twilight years, but we speak so little of the middle, where most of our lives are spent. For many of us, nothing so grand as even a midlife crisis materializes. There is just the great slog of carrying on without losing one's nerve.

I had not arrived as a pilgrim to Copacabana, but, in being someone who also had something to ask of life, I became one. I asked that my novel find a publisher. "If it comes true," my new friend said with a grin, "you'll have to come back, you know?"

Mongolia

I GREW UP in India with all the major world religions. I attended a Christian boarding school in a Hindu-majority country that is roughly tied with Pakistan for the second-largest Muslim population in the world. My mother's family were Sikhs, and I counted among my closest friends a Jew from Bombay and Buddhists from Tibet. Pilgrimage is common to all these faiths, even as it is utterly distinctive in each. In Islam, the pilgrimage to Mecca is an ordained pillar of faith that the Prophet Muhammad performed himself. In Christianity, the culture of cherishing relics and visiting holy places is said to have begun with Saint Helena—the mother of Constantine I, the first Roman emperor to convert to Christianity in 312— rushing off to the Holy Land in search of the True Cross.

Some pilgrimages enshrine sorrow, like the Ashura in Iraq, which would be the last stop on my journey; others, like fiesta in Bolivia's Copacabana, are pilgrimages of joy and rapture. Some are historical, like the Jewish commemoration of exile; others, like the Mecca pilgrimage, represent the repurposing of an older sanctity, in this case that of pre-Islamic Arabia. In India, which has some of the greatest scenes of pilgrimage anywhere in the world, such as the Kumbh Mela, where every twelve years the largest gathering of humanity on earth—more than 100 million—comes together at the confluence of the Ganges and Yamuna Rivers, I had also witnessed the touching intimacy of a family or group of friends who set out for a holy place on a Sunday, just as someone might go fishing or to a national park in the United States.

It was the ordinariness of this latter kind of pilgrimage, away from the grand spectacles of Ashura and fiesta, that I had hoped to capture in Buddhist Mongolia. I had imagined springtime pilgrimages, people visiting monasteries as the weather warmed. If La Paz is the highest capital in the world, Ulaanbaatar is the coldest, with January temperatures reaching minus thirty degrees. In fact, even as I was setting out at the end of May, my guide and translator, Orgilbaatar Tsolmon, who goes by Orgil, was sending me videos of snow showers in the Mongolian capital.

My flight from New York connected through Istanbul; the first leg was ten hours, and from there we flew another eight hours in a level line across the face of Asia. The Black Sea gave way to the Caspian and, beyond, to a land of mountain, desert, and steppe. The Mongols, led by Genghis Khan and his descendants, poured over the steppe in the thirteenth century and, in the words of the eighteenth-century British historian Edward Gibbon, "the caliphs fell, and the Caesars trembled on their throne," even as representatives of the major faiths—from Islam and Nestorian Christianity to Taoism and myriad forms of Buddhism—would come before the great khans to make their case for why their particular creed ought to be the official religion of the empire.

My first glimpse of Mongolia was of rolling hills draped in thin emerald grass, of cloud shadows the size of lakes, and of raking beams of morning light breaking through a heavy sky. "Nomadism," I scribbled in my notebook in a sleepless haze, "captures the very spiritual heart of pilgrimage, which is to wander." If the Latin *peregrinus* gives us *pilgrim*, it also gives us *peregrination*.

Orgil was waiting for me at Chinggis Khaan International Airport in Ulaanbaatar with a red Nissan SUV. My first thought on seeing him, with his long hair and light beard, was of the Nepalese artist Araniko's late thirteenth-century rendering of Kublai Khan, Genghis Khan's grandson. "In Xanadu, did Kubla Khan / A stately pleasure-dome decree . . ." The Coleridge poem was the first I had committed to memory as a child, during a blackout in Delhi, but Kublai was more than the figment of an opium dream. He founded the Yuan dynasty (1279–1368) in China and established Beijing (then known as Dadu) as its capital, and was the man whose conversion to Buddhism around 1258 brought shamanic Mongolia into the orbit of Tibetan Buddhism.

The influence of Buddhism grew sporadically for almost

seven centuries in Mongolia, merging in profound ways with its ancient worship of nature—of mountains, water, the eternal blue sky. But then, in the early decades of the twentieth century, Buddhism encountered a mortal enemy: Soviet-backed Communism. The great majority of the country's monastic institutions were leveled to the ground; some eighteen thousand monks were killed; and, in a society where about one-third of the adult male population were lamas (though not all living in monasteries), Buddhism was ripped out root and branch.

In 1990, with the fall of Communism, religious freedom was established in Mongolia and Buddhism was allowed to be practiced again. My first destination was the Khamar Monastery, three hundred miles south in the Gobi Desert, which had been all but destroyed in 1938. It was said to be situated at one of the portals to Shambhala—a mythical kingdom of peace and tranquility in the Buddhist imagining—and had been founded in the century before by an artist, saint, and sybarite called Danzanravjaa, or Ravjaa, known as the lama of the Gobi. Bolivia had given me new respect for the survival of the sacred, despite great political and historical upheavals, and I was curious to see what pilgrimage would look like in a place where it had been stamped out for generations—curious to see the old pilgrim routes leading back to the locus of sanctity, like neural pathways reforming around an area of trauma.

MONGOLIA, BROADLY SPEAKING, is a country with half the landmass of India and a population smaller than that of Los Angeles proper—some 3.3 million people—of which about half live in Ulaanbaatar alone. As we left the capital's new Japanese-built airport armed with supplies of chips, Snickers, Coke Zeros, and vodka as offerings, I gained a first impression of an unnerving emptiness. After some initial settlements of white yurts, or *gers*, as they're known here, and houses with brightly colored corrugated roofs behind dark wooden stockades, all signs of habitation fell away. On that morning in late May, spectral wisps of snow blew over the long two-lane highway, and the wind was so strong that I found it difficult to put my jacket on outside the car.

Amid what seemed like trackless wastes, there periodically appeared the giant ragged form of an *ovoo*, or cairn. Its beanpole of a body was bandaged in blue *khadags* (prayer scarves), its stony mound of a base littered with vodka bottles and the occasional skull of a dead animal. The ovoo is a monument to the spirits of the natural world, known here as *nagas* and *savdags*. Orgil, following the custom of honoring these easily offended beings, lest they punish you for your neglect, honked three times as we went by. "This is the Gen Z way," he said, grinning, "but I prefer the old way," which involves circling the ovoo on foot three times in a clockwise motion.

But it was too cold to stop. It was too cold to smoke, too cold to take a pee. The temperature was only in the low thirties, but the wind bit through me, and it was hard to believe that this was a relatively mild spring day by Mongolian standards. Outside Choir, a dust-bitten town halfway to the monastery, we inhaled a lunch of mutton broth and dumplings, fried rice and a meat-stuffed pastry called a *khuushuur*. Then we drove on, another four hours. The land turned arid and flat. Double-humped Bactrian camels appeared along the side of the road. An enticing band of opalescent sky offered the relief of a horizon after hours of rain and snow.

Orgil, in between telling me of his days in a metal band, when "I drank beers left and right," would occasionally grow serious. "During Communism," he said, "we lost our national identity." The purges of the 1930s plundered the country's monasteries and temples—there had been some seven hundred in the nineteenth century—which Orgil described as repositories of folklore, history, traditional medicine, and learning. Mongolia, after winning independence from Qing China in 1911, began those early decades of the twentieth century as a feudal theocracy with a godlike figure, akin to the Dalai Lama, called the Bogd Khan, at its helm, overseeing around eighty thousand monks. (The Dalai Lama recently introduced a Mongolian child as the tenth reincarnation of the Bogd.) "They shot all the head lamas," Orgil said. "They murdered all the teachers." The fires from the monasteries were rumored to have burned for weeks. Christopher Kaplonski, a social anthropologist who has conducted research in Mongolia, has written that, though the total number of Mongolians killed between 1937 and 1939 is unknown, "credible estimates range from 35,000 to 45,000."

As evening fell, we arrived at the ger camp on the edge of the Gobi, a short drive from the Khamar Monastery. We were the only ones there. Orgil had made me worried that there would be no pilgrims at all. Bolivia was a lesson in the imperishability of the sacred, but it had also shown me how places of pilgrimage, like the sacred crag on the Island of the Sun, could die. If you ban a religion for more than half a century, murder its clergy, and raze its monasteries, as the Communists had in Mongolia, then maybe you do deal it a death blow?

I was full of dark thoughts when the ger camp began magically to fill. I'd just finished a dinner of *banshtai tsai*, dumplings in a goat milk and tea broth, and retired to my ger, where I was watching the wood-burning stove cast shadows on the wooden lattice and felt walls, when I heard electronic music blaring into the Gobi. I stepped outside to see the neat rows of gers now brightly lit, noise and chatter pouring out of their doorways. Bottles of soda were being ferried back and forth and mixed with vodka. Prim, lightly made-up girls sat on the edges of what looked like the Mongolian equivalent of a frat party. "Who are these people?" I asked Orgil in amazement. "Pilgrims," he answered. Some were part of a construction company, others students with exams on the horizon. They had come to draw energy from Shambhala. The rites the next morning were to begin before dawn, yet the pilgrim parties, with their Chaucerian feeling of intimacy among strangers, continued raucously into the night.

Just before daybreak, at 4:20 a.m., we joined a cavalcade of SUVs off-roading through the desert, drawing ruby-red parabolas over the dunes. Our first stop was a fertility shrine near the monastery. On a hill were two mounds of sand and rock with stone finials, connected by a beam that was wrapped in the blue prayer cloths. Women in puffer jackets with cartons of milk went back and forth between the shrine and the edge of the hill, casting their offerings of milk into the air. Orgil told me that no man could perform the rite unless his mother had died in the past forty-nine days, in which case he could perform it on behalf of her spirit.

The sun rose over the Gobi, showing reddish earth and black-edged dunes. The sky was a cold, motionless blue. While the women performed the ritual, I spoke to a group of men in their late thirties and early forties who worked for a real estate company in Ulaanbaatar. One was an economist, another a lawyer, a third a businessman. They had arrived by train from the capital. "I came here to recharge my energy and cleanse my spirit," said Egi, the economist. (Mongolians use patronymics rather than Western-style surnames; in conversation, people often go by just one name.) "This place is a world energy center." When I asked if the ritual had been handed down to him by his parents, he said, "They knew about it, but they were not authorized to come. We are the lucky generation." He added: "This Shambhala reminds us that we are not just ordinary nomads. We had an enlightened one [Danzanravjaa] live among us." Since the transition to the democratic era, Egi said, "Mongolian people have come to know that we have a great religious and cultural heritage."

Munkhdul, the businessman, said in halting English, "It's a reconnection in modern times to the past of our life." Some moments later, our band of pilgrims (about fifty to one hundred) reconvened outside the gateway to the Shambhala complex, where a pair of mesmeric half-closed eyes, painted on a wall of pinkish orange, gazed out at us, symbolizing the inward-turned sagacity of the Buddha. Stepping across the threshold, we found ourselves in a rectangular enclosure of red earth marked out by a perimeter of white stupas. It was like being in a Zen garden, where one proceeded from one station to another, performing a series of rituals and rites under an open sky. In the distance, the level sands of the Gobi fell away as far as the eye could see. It was an austere, heart-stopping glimpse of the void.

Our guide, Haidav, was from the Gobi region. In his early thirties now, he had been selected as a boy by Gandantegchinlen (often referred to simply as Gandan), the country's main monastery in Ulaanbaatar, to spend four years in the southern Indian state of Karnataka, where, at a center of Tibetan Buddhism—the Namdroling Monastery, popularly known as the Golden Temple—he had been educated in the religion of his forefathers with the express aim of reintroducing it to Mongolia. As he led us into the Shambhala, he seemed less like a guide than like a monk reeducating his countrymen about a faith whose core precepts, such as the belief in karma and reincarnation, had survived the ravages of Communism but whose rituals had to be relearned from scratch. Our group was composed almost entirely of Mongolians, but no one knew what to do at the various stations any more than I did.

At the genie's belly, a low mound of dark rocks, Haidav told us to exhale all of our sins and bad thoughts, intentional and unintentional. At the site of Danzanravjaa's ger, which was just a circle in the sand, we offered handfuls of grain. We wished that "with the help of the enlightened one, we would be reborn into the Shambhala." Then we went to three other circles representing past, present, and future. Haidav told us to walk not through but around them. We had open bottles of vodka in our hands and made offerings into the air. (Milk and vodka! It was a combination I would encounter time and again in this nomadic post-Soviet society.) Haidav told us not to wish for money or material things but only that which was regenerative—a child, rain, or power. He placed a special emphasis on looking in, on harmony and balance. He said that all the bad things that happen to us, whether ill health or failure in our careers, were emanations of what was within and, in cleansing the inner sphere, we could succeed in the outer.

If pilgrimage is exteriorized mysticism, a way for human beings to grasp spiritual truths, the Shambhala felt almost like a cosmogram or mandala, a metaphysical scheme writ small. We came to a circle of red rocks that was the energy heart of the whole enclosure. Here, we sat down. Some lay on the rocks and rolled from side to side. The aim was to draw in the energy of the place. I talked to Samdanbazar, a seventy-eight-year-old herder from Töv Province, in the environs of Ulaanbaatar. She wore a gold-and-purple *deel*, a long coat of sorts, fur lined in the winter, with tiny earrings, her dyed hair whitening at the roots. Watching her roll back and forth, taking such obvious pleasure in the rite, I had to ask what it had been like to be denied all this for the first forty-five years of her life. "We had to hide everything," she said. "My father was a lama, so we had to hide our *thangkas* [Tibetan Buddhist cloth paintings], Buddhas, and religious artifacts."

Our last station was the Golden Skull Hill, where a central ovoo overlooked the desert beyond. There we chanted, "*Um sain amgalan boltugai*"—"may there be peace with you"—and sang "Ulemjiin Chanar" ("Perfect Qualities"), a Mongolian folk song that Danzanravjaa had composed himself. Haidav was almost scolding in the care with which he instructed us to sing as a chorus. "Whatever your failures," he said at the end of our morning at the Shambhala, "it's because of your mind."

THE EMPHASIS ON interiority, on isolating the self as the site for spiritual advancement and failure, felt very different from the Christian pilgrimage in Bolivia. The focus there had been outward: on Mary, her miracles, on what she could give you. Here, almost everyone spoke of enlightenment from within and of certain corrosive human emotions, anger being among the gravest of them, that would impede that progress. In Mongolia, the texture of sin felt less like a crime against God than against oneself. Three symbols are often associated with Danzanravjaa's life and thought: a female figure representing his love of pleasure; a swan symbolizing the arts; and, lastly, a scorpion signifying the human potential for self-destructiveness. Outside our ger camp, there was a giant metal sculpture of a black scorpion, its tail raised, surrounded by desert sands on all sides. It stood as a reminder of the cardinal sin in the Buddhist scheme: rage, which, like the myth of the scorpion, makes us our own worst enemies, liable to sting ourselves in the head.

It was Haidav who first told me of the family of priests who had taken a solemn vow in 1856 to preserve the artifacts of Ravjaa, even as I had grown more interested in the role of relics in pilgrimage after witnessing the power of Yupanqui's Virgin in Bolivia.

At 7:00 a.m., on my last morning in the Gobi, I met

Altan-Ochir Altangarel, seventh in the line of priests who had sworn to be protectors of Ravjaa's possessions, outside the Danzanravjaa Museum in the desert town of Sainshand. I had not expected the living descendant of Ravjaa's nineteenth-century trustee to be dressed like a Brooklyn hipster. He was in his early thirties, in skinny black jeans, with vintage glasses framing his arresting blue eyes. If the dharma of Altan-Ochir's family was to protect Ravjaa's relics, it had been tested to the extreme. Altan-Ochir's great-grandfather was arrested by the Communists. When he got out, he hid Ravjaa's things in the desert. The location was neither written down nor revealed to anyone save Altan-Ochir's father (Zoldon) who was told in 1965, when he was five. Zoldon learned the mantras and sutras (sacred texts) in secret. "He would hide his incense stick in a cigarette," Altan-Ochir said. When Communism fell, Ravjaa's artifacts were recovered and housed in the museum we were in. It was an extremely rare instance of Mongolian Buddhism recovering the rich material culture it had lost, and it begged the question of why a religion so disdainful of the material world as Buddhism should fetishize relics, here the tooth of the Buddha, there Ravjaa's possessions. "The first thing of anything is materialistic," Altan-Ochir answered easily, "but turning the materialistic thing into wisdom is the key to Buddhism." What was true of relics was true of pilgrimage, too. "Human beings are pretty unique," Altan-Ochir said, with a smile, as if aware that the curated walk through the Shambhala was a mere instrument of inner realization. "They always need to do something to truly believe. The Shambhala allows them to do that."

I rose to leave. Altan-Ochir asked I light seven brass lamps to honor our meeting, then, in a jade cup that had belonged to Ravjaa, he poured out some holy water that was infused ever so slightly with the milk-distilled vodka Mongolians cherish. With this, Orgil and I took our leave, speeding out of the desert into the steppe beyond.

KUBLAI KHAN MAY have laid the foundation for the rise of Tibetan Buddhism in Mongolia, but it was a man called Zanabazar—a monk, scholar, and artist—who solidified its position. In everything from scripture to ritual, temple design, and even religious fashion, including monastic robes with blue cuffs evoking the blue sky that Genghis Khan claimed to worship, the hand of Zanabazar is visible.

At the Erdene Zuu Monastery, founded by Zanabazar's great-grandfather in the sixteenth century after the declaration of Tibetan Buddhism as the state religion of Mongolia, I witnessed an amazing scene, proof of the cocktail of motives that puts us on the road to pilgrimage. Erdene Zuu, with its green-tiled roofs in the Chinese style, is Mongolia's oldest monastery, built in 1586. It is also located near the ruins of the Mongol capital at Karakorum, about 530 miles from Khamar Monastery. On entering Erdene Zuu's vast, grassy complex, with its perimeter wall crenelated with white stupas and nothing but big sky on all sides, I felt the spirit of a Mongolian camp. Nomadism harbors a disdain for materiality, yet it was hard not to feel myself on consecrated ground, even if only in historical terms. It was mainly from here that the descendants of Genghis Khan in the thirteenth century brought the world to its knees, from present-day Ukraine to Korea. The site had more recent memories, too. Of its sixty-two temples and some five hundred facilities, the vast majority had been destroyed during the ravages of the 1930s. All around me, amid a handful of stupas and temples, were the flattened foundations of buildings in the religious complex. There had been fifteen hundred lamas here in the nineteenth century; there were fewer than fifty today. At the entrance, I spoke briefly to Mandakhtsog Monkhbaatar, who was in his early twenties, dressed in orange-and-red robes with those huge turquoise cuffs and high boots with blue piping. Like Haidav, he had spent years studying at the Golden Temple monastery in India, relearning the traditions that Communism had left Mongolian Buddhism too depleted to teach. Monkhbaatar's great-grandfather had been a prominent lama in the southwestern province of Bayankhongor. When I asked the young monk about him, he said casually, "He was murdered," then rushed into the great complex, where the morning chants were set to begin.

A plump child lama in a plumed yellow cap appeared on the wooden watchtower of a temple whose sloping white facade evoked the Potala in Lhasa, Tibet—the winter palace of the Dalai Lamas. A conch shell sounded three times. Knots of pilgrims and tourists milling about outside drew near. Inside, monks sat chanting on wooden benches in a blue-ceilinged room hung with thangkas. Sutras wrapped in yellow silk rotated on a turnstile. As bells and chanting reached a crescendo, amid clouds of incense, a woman in a black-and-copper deel, her schoolteacher's face tremulous with ardor, came rushing in. She then began to perform full-bodied prostrations in the aisle between the monks, some chanting, others laughing or charging their phones. Again and again, as the tempo rose around her, this thin, bespectacled woman prostrated herself in ecstasy, doing what is known in Sanskrit as *ashtanga pranam*, or the eight-body-part salute: hands, feet, knees, chest, and chin. Watching her, I was reminded of a pilgrim I had once seen at a shrine in central India. He had looked like a bureaucrat or bank clerk, the ordinariness of his appearance only amplifying the extraordinariness of his actions. I'd watched him take a rock and place it on the floor a few feet away and then lie flat on the ground face down and wriggle his way toward it. He'd repeated the same gesture several times until he circled the shrine. "This," the young Brahmin whom I'd been traveling with said to me, "is *bhava*" (a kind of rapture). Later, I learned that the woman at Erdene Zuu was a forty-year-old herder from Inner Mongolia, the region of the country that had remained part of China after present-day (Outer) Mongolia won its independence in 1911. She told me that she'd been a devout Buddhist since she was a child. "It's the most perfect religion because it enlightens from within," she said. But it wasn't just Buddha who had brought her to Erdene Zuu. She said she came for Genghis Khan, too. "He was our ancestor," she said of the founder of the Mongol Empire—who was not Buddhist but shamanic. "I wanted to receive the particular energy of this man here, in what was the capital of the Mongol Empire and of Buddhism."

"So is this a religious pilgrimage for you, or a nationalistic one?" I asked.

"It is both," she said. "For Mongolians, this is a sacred place. This is ancestral land." When I asked her if she felt Chinese at all, she said, "I'm 100 percent Mongol, even if I live in the part that's China. We may live in different locations, but that doesn't change the fact that we're all Mongols."

When I asked for her contact details, she demurred, explaining that to share them was unsafe. Then, as I was walking away, she came rushing after me, imploring me not to post the pictures we had taken together on any social media or mention her by name in whatever I wrote. It was a reminder that political peril had always been part of the calculus of pilgrimage, whether in the Middle Ages, when Islam's conquest of the Holy Land gave rise to local shrines, such as Santiago de Compostela and Canterbury, or now, for this pilgrimage-within-a-pilgrimage of a Mongolian herder, honoring her ethnic and spiritual ancestor, irrespective of any national boundary.

Growing up in India, I witnessed the intersection of religion and nationalism canalized into a militarized form of pilgrimage. In 1990, the Hindu nationalist leader L. K. Advani led a *ratha yatra*, or "chariot pilgrimage," from Somnath temple in the western state of Gujarat, where a major Hindu temple saw the first of many assaults upon it in the eleventh century. The yatra, steeped in historical pain and revenge, was headed for the city of Ayodhya, a thousand miles away in Uttar Pradesh, where a sixteenth-century mosque—named after the Emperor Babur, who, incidentally, was a descendant of

Genghis Khan and the founder of the Mughal (derived from Mongol) dynasty—stood on the alleged site of what was the birthplace of the Hindu god Ram. The yatra was stopped before it got to Ayodhya, and Advani arrested, but the rage he had tapped into was not so easily contained. Two years later, on December 6, 1992, a mob of *kar sevaks*, or religious volunteers, some coming as pilgrims with bricks for the construction of a new temple, destroyed the mosque. Religious riots ensued, and hundreds died. Ayodhya was the crucible that led to the ascendancy of Hindu nationalism in India. Two decades on, it gave rise to the majoritarian politics of Narendra Modi. Pilgrimage offered a release from the monotony of daily life, but it also galvanized people in the service of faith, often at the expense of other faiths—and over such an enterprise, of people sent away from home with their hearts full of religious zeal, there forever hung the specter of a crusade.

ORGIL AND I drove some fifteen hundred miles in five days, off-roading over what felt like the spine of Asia: valleys of spring flowers with ancient burial sites encircled by gently creased hills of green velvet. Orgil let me drive. The full expanse of the steppe, streaked with islands of shadow, opened up around us. Sometimes the sky would darken and a storm would roll in, turning the furrowed hills a morose green; then a herd of semi-wild, rain-drenched horses might assemble at the center of the road. I had never seen such emptiness. I felt myself in a country where animals outnumbered people many times over. It was as exhilarating as it was disquieting—the solitary sight of a ger in the distance, the cattle-covered crest of a hill dotted black, beige, and white, as if the fickle hand of nature had taken up pointillism. It was easy to imagine this changeless landscape as one where people were especially attuned to the spirits of the natural world. "Throughout Mongolia it is believed," Orgil said, "that if you pollute the water, the savdag will be angry at you, so we don't even pour milk into the water, which we consider to be the purest thing." That shamanic worship had fertilized Mongolian Buddhism, giving it its distinct character, which in turn, because of the influence of Tibetan Buddhism, already included certain esoteric teachings, practices, and rituals, known in classical India as the Tantras.

I hardly saw Ulaanbaatar until the end of my time in Mongolia. The location of the capital once known to Mongols as Khuree, meaning "monastery," and later to the Russians as Urga, had not been fixed until the late 1700s and, even today, the city of nearly 1.7 million has the air of a giant encampment. A suburban sprawl of ger neighborhoods—ramshackle houses and yurts—surround a Soviet-style city center of decaying apartment blocks and bureaucratic behemoths touched up with blue glass and steel.

Here, the Gandan Monastery, the de facto Vatican of Mongolian Buddhism, was the only such institution allowed to remain partially open during Communism. Although it was closed during the purges of the late 1930s, Munkhbaatar Batchuluun, forty-five, a jovial lama who handled communications for the monastery, explained that it owed its survival to a cynical act of tokenism. Henry Wallace, Franklin

D. Roosevelt's vice president at the time, was in Mongolia on a fact-finding mission in 1944, and the Communist government wanted to show that some modicum of religious freedom existed in Mongolia. Thus the Gandan, though hollowed out, was permitted to stay open as a Potemkin monastery. Mongolia had come as close as any society to having eradicated a religious way of life, with deep roots in the social fabric, yet here, too, as so often on this pilgrimage of mine, the sacred had triumphed in the end. The newly built main hall of the Gandan was swarming once more with pilgrims and lamas. The recitation of the sacred Ganjuur sutra—a practice that had been repressed in Mongolia for decades, the renewal of which I was there to witness—was underway. Sitting in the coffee shop downstairs, in a building that was a teeming complex of ATMs, broadcast studios, and what Munkhbaatar referred to as "donation receiving desks," akin to cashiers at a bank, for the performance of various religious services, he described Buddhism as never really lost "but preserved in the minds of people."

As a boy in the countryside in the 1980s, he recalled his grandfather—a lama who disrobed after the execution of his teacher—performing Buddhist rites under cover of darkness at an altar he kept hidden in his home behind a curtain. The other villagers, who praised Communist ideals of progress by day, would by night call on his grandfather, the disrobed lama, to perform healing rites. The Buddha outlined three freedoms, Munkhbaatar explained, of behavior, speech, and mind: "The Communists controlled the first two, but they could not control our minds," he said.

On my penultimate night in Ulaanbaatar, I went to meet a woman named Gerelmaa, who went by Giimaa for short, for a shamanic ceremony. She lived in a ger neighborhood in a small house, with a yard full of rubble and rotting armchairs. A white Hyundai sat on cinder blocks, framed against the setting sun. Giimaa, a stout chain smoker in her sixties with a single upper tooth, had been an East German–trained electrical engineer under Communism before becoming a shaman in 1991. She'd often travel up to five thousand miles a year on pilgrimages to Uvs Province in the west of the country to draw energy from the place where one of her ancestors, a powerful shaman in his day, had once lived. As we sat in an upstairs room full of taxidermic birds of prey, she told me that she mostly uses her shamanic powers to help people cure illnesses and dispel dark energy.

Giimaa donned her heavy reindeer-skin coat, hung with a bear's foot, a vulture's claw, a wolf's paw, and brightly colored tassels. She made offerings of milk and vodka, which her spirit, like those of most people in Mongolia, seemed to relish. With a veil over her face and feathers on her head, she began to beat a pentagonal drum, dancing about the small room.

Once the spirit took hold, Giimaa slumped down on the floor and began to speak in the gravelly voice of her male ancestor. She had told me not to be scared, but it was scary. The spirit asked about my life, and I gave him the salient details: I was the love child of a Pakistani politician and an Indian journalist. My father had been assassinated by his own bodyguard. I was married to a man from Tennessee and had been unable to return to India to see my family since 2019, when Modi's government had stripped me of my overseas citizenship only months after I wrote an article critical of his reelection.

The spirit saw darkness in my life. He asked me to envision my home in the United States and, touching me, flew there to dispel that dark energy. My mind zoomed up, too, giving me an aerial view of this scene of a shamanic ceremony in a little house with the sun setting over the hills surrounding Ulaanbaatar. I thought of my fellow pilgrims: Eduardo Quintela, and his quiet tribute to his father; Aracely Alcón, full of gratitude for Santiago's restored mobility; and the woman at Erdene Zuu on her perilous journey.

Pilgrimage in that moment seemed less to me like exteriorized mysticism and more a rite of remembrance. The world would have us forget what is painful. It would have us move on and be free of the past; but both as individuals and societies, we have our loyalties to what we have known and endured. Pilgrimage gave us the illusion of a forward movement across space, even as it allowed an inner journey toward communion with our past. It was a crystallization of the poet Joseph Brodsky's idea that "if there is any substitute for love, it's memory."

Iraq

GRIEF, MEMORY, LOVE. I had not planned for this trinity of themes to become the substratum of my pilgrimage. Yet six months on, to arrive in Iraq in the nights leading up to Ashura—the climactic tenth day in a ritual period of mourning for the world's more than 150 million Shiite Muslims—was to be confronted by a grief so fresh that the event that inspired it, the martyrdom of the Prophet Muhammad's grandson Hussein in 680, might have occurred yesterday.

In July, William Keo, a twenty-seven-year-old French Cambodian photographer, and I flew into the holy city of Najaf, 110 miles south of Baghdad, arriving just after 9:00 p.m. We were met at the airport by Khuder al-Harooni, our guide and translator, an avuncular figure in his midfifties. Driving in from the airport, we watched the modern city of Najaf fall away in a blur of overpasses, brightly lit shops and restaurants, and a headlight parade of white sedans. Outside the pedestrianized medieval center of town—where our hotel was situated—our taxi stopped in a sea of black. It was as if the whole city of 1 million were in mourning. "The ladies, too," Khuder said, pointing to a group of women in abayas. The majority, though, were beautifully barbered young men in long robes, many with hipster haircuts and beards trimmed at the chin, all making their way to the center of the shrine city. A motorbike with two men riding pillion swerved to a stop in front of us. It had small red-and-black flags on its handlebars. The green letters in Arabic script read LABAIK, YA HUSSEIN ("I am here, O Hussein").

To be Shiite was to live with the pain, never more acute than at Ashura, of not having been there for Hussein when it mattered most. In 680, Hussein had hearkened to the call of Muslims in the garrison town of Kufa, a few miles east of Najaf. His grandfather the Prophet had been dead for less than fifty years. In that time, the small community of believers had grown into the vast Arab Muslim empire. Hussein's father,

Ali—the Prophet's beloved son-in-law and cousin—was the last of the four Rashidun ("rightly guided") caliphs until he died in 661 at the hands of an assassin who struck him with a poisoned sword as he prayed. The Shiat Ali (Partisans of Ali) were at first merely his followers, people who believed that the mantle of the Prophet could be assumed only by one of his bloodline. So when, in 680, Muawiya, the first caliph since Ali, died and the caliphate passed to his dissolute son, Yazid, the Shiat Ali implored Hussein to take his rightful place at the head of Islam.

He would have believed he was defending the true faith of his father and grandfather when he rode out from Medina, in present-day Saudi Arabia, with seventy-two of his companions, to the plain of Karbala, fifty miles north of Najaf. On the way, many tried to dissuade him, telling him that "though the heart of the city [of Kufa] is with thee, its sword is against thee," but he rode on, like a man running to meet his destiny—a Christlike figure who sought to redeem the religion of his grandfather by forfeiting his life. At Karbala, Hussein found himself quite alone. Yazid, having subjected the living descendants of the Prophet Muhammad to days of heat and thirst, slaughtered them in a massacre that traumatized Sunni and Shiite alike. The main difference was that the Sunnis, who today are a vast majority of 1.9 billion Muslims, were able to move on, whereas the Shiites dedicated themselves to bearing witness to Hussein's sacrifice—the word for martyr in Arabic, *shahid*, like the Greek *martur*, means "witness."

The mourning for Hussein was a dramatization of a historical wound. It gave Shiite Islam, with its origin in pain and defeat, an entirely different complexion from its Sunni coeval, which was energized by the political triumphs of that first century of Islam after the Prophet's death, when the entire classical world, from India to Spain, succumbed to the new empire of faith. The split between Shiite and Sunni started as partisanship over who should succeed the Prophet. After Karbala, it hardened into something of a schism, even though the relationship between the two strains of belief was more symbiotic than mutually exclusive.

NAJAF ON THAT first night was like a town preparing for a medieval battle. We entered on foot through narrow side streets with knife sharpeners at every corner, whetstones crackling and sparking. Broad-bellied iron vats on low blue gas fires held vast quantities of rice and *qeema*, a spiced stew of meat and chickpeas made especially at Ashura. We dropped our bags at the hotel and walked into the floodlit precincts of the shrine of Imam Ali. A siren sounded, as if summoning soldiers to their stations. The dandyish men I had seen earlier stood in a line on a red carpet, brandishing swords in long, sweeping movements. Farther along, in an arena of sorts, the neighborhoods of Najaf were marching in procession, bearing banners, coats of arms, and liquid-eyed images of Hussein wearing a dark, youthful beard and a green turban. At the center of each procession, a strongman carried a *mashael* (iron chandelier) on his muscular shoulders, its twenty-seven flaming lamps doused in crude oil. He plowed it into the crowd like a battering ram, wielding it around and around to the sound of drums, cheers, and an excited cleric speaking into a microphone like a sportscaster. The crowd eddied, some with batons dancing concentrically around the wheel of fire, others collecting around two young men in white. They had cut their heads in a ritual called *tatbir*, and their faces were streaming with blood. As the tempo rose, a perimeter of cellphone screens formed around them. The modern technology, with its direct link to social media, amplified certain elements of bravado and exhibitionism that were already part of the performance. One of the men, bearded and handsome, who looked as if he might be in his early twenties, fell to his knees and sliced at his bleeding head with the two daggers he carried in his hands, as if he'd meant to scalp himself. "We have come to return the sacrifice of Imam Hussein," said the eighteen-year-old friend of the man on his knees, by way of explanation of his actions to me. "Imam Ali was killed by the sword. Now we remember their sacrifices."

I had been on the ground in Najaf for less than two hours, having flown sixteen from New York. The heat, the swords, the blood, the air thick with the stench of oil—it was overwhelming. Khuder, sensing my fatigue and alarm, said, "All this was banned under Saddam, so the people are starved for such festivals." Looking around, I realized that most of these men could not have been even a few years old when Saddam Hussein fell in 2003.

As we took a break on a quieter street leading away from Bab al-Tusi, the northern archway of the shrine, illuminated red that night, we came across a small stampede in the courtyard of a mosque. A young boy in a gold tunic and a green spiked helmet, astride a white horse, was surrounded by a crowd of older men. He was meant to be Qasim, Imam Hussein's teenage nephew, Khuder explained. "Will I also be among the martyrs?" he had asked his uncle before riding out to his death.

Najaf had its own version of Bolivia's prestes, honored members of the citizenry who funded and organized service stations for pilgrims called *mawkib*s. Some provided food and water, others street theater and rites of mourning for Hussein. At one such mawkib, run by a black-turbaned cleric—the color denoting descent from the Prophet—I met Yasir Yaseen, a twenty-three-year-old medical student from Najaf who lives in Istanbul and had returned to his hometown for Ashura. He had a light beard and a smile that exposed uneven teeth. He said that each night from now until Ashura was dedicated to a different episode in the reenactment of the tragedy of Hussein, which was a procession of deaths—those of Hussein's son (Ali Akbar), his nephew (Qasim), his half brother (Abbas), his six-month-old baby (Ali Asghar), and others—culminating in that of Hussein himself. Looking down at the rectangle of men at our feet, many of whom had removed their black shirts and were thumping their bare chests in a slow, hypnotic movement, Yaseen, perhaps afraid I would misunderstand, said, "We're not hurting ourselves for nothing. Fourteen hundred years ago, Imam Hussein went for something, and we were not with him, so one of the things we say during this period is '*Ya letna kona ma'km,*' 'We wish we were with you.'"

Penance has always been a key element of pilgrimage. All major religious cultures use physical endurance and even pain as a conduit to draw closer to God. In Bolivia, some pilgrims made the approach to the shrine on their knees. Francisco Goya's *A Procession of Flagellants*, painted between 1808 and 1812, shows figures in white with conical hats beating their own backs with flails. In India, I had seen exquisite examples of the mortification of flesh, almost as if it were necessary to negate the body for the spirit to speak. What made Ashura unique was its use of theater to create a two-planed reality: we were both in the present, mourning the past, and with Hussein circa 680 on the plain of Karbala. Pilgrimage is nothing if not a spectacle, here in the dances for the Virgin of Copacabana, there in the different stations of remembrance at the Shambhala, surrounded by the drama of the Gobi on all sides. In Najaf, I felt part of an immersive street theater that erased the line between audience and actor and used the short plays unfolding around us to bring about that original Greek sense of catharsis as a cleansing or purification for our complicity in the events of the past.

A likely apocryphal story states that Qasim had been betrothed to Hussein's daughter on the eve of the battle, and, at one mawkib, hundreds of young men under satin flags of black, green, and red edged in gold sang to the poem "Groom of Karbala." "This is a bride of sacrifice, a bride of blood," Khuder translated. A cleric on the stage began the verse, and the young men, some carrying flowers in their hands, saluting in time to the music, sang the chorus back—"Beautiful as Joseph, this Lion of Karbala"—a cappella, their voices carrying up into the night air. The sight was mesmerizing. "They didn't know Saddam's persecution," Wissam al-Turfi, an older man managing the crowd at the mawkib, told me, scanning the expanse of intent faces, "but their parents told them about it."

Given my experience of Mongolia, where Communism had driven Buddhism underground, and where the cycle of erasure and return was still playing out, I was curious to know what that persecution had looked like. "We still met," al-Turfi said, "but in secret," adding that not all displays of religion were suppressed under Saddam—it was the Shiite outpourings of passion around Ashura and Arbaeen, the commemoration of Hussein's martyrdom that occurs forty days later and entails a fifty-mile walk from Najaf to Karbala, that were banned. "What was Saddam so afraid of?" I asked.

"Imam Hussein," al-Turfi said. "Imam Hussein is revolution."

WE HAD BEEN out all night, walking the streets of Najaf. As this last gathering broke up, plastic containers of freshly cooked qeema and rice began circulating. It was nearly dawn by the time we returned to the hotel.

When I woke at noon, it was 115 degrees outside and getting hotter. Looking out through an inch-wide opening in the heavy curtains, I saw a beige, treeless city of red plastic water tanks, cluttered rooftops, and telephone towers. Our hotel was full of pilgrims. In the elevator, I met a Kuwaiti who said he had come to Iraq to witness the *museebat*, or "tribulations," of Hussein. Downstairs, the lobby was packed with members of the mercantile South Asian community of Bohras, who were also part of the Shiite fold. The men wore gold and white, the women bright two-piece garments consisting of hooded smocks and skirts, the hem of one matching the hem of the other.

The Shiite world is wide and various. There were the Ismailis in South Asia and Tajikistan, Zaidis in Yemen, and Alevis and Alawites in Anatolia and Syria. Each group took a different line on succession to the Prophet, and each had a different focus of devotion, but none was indifferent to Ali. It is hard to overstate the mystical power of Ali as a counterpoint to Muhammad, not just within Shiite Islam but in Islam more generally. "His refusal to play the dirty game of tribal power politics," writes Barnaby Rogerson in *The Heirs of the Prophet Muhammad* (2006), "would always have frustrated him from becoming an effective political leader of the Arabs. . . . Ali is testimony to the fact that the most beautiful ideals must perish in the sordid world of human politics."

Ali is my middle name. It was given to me by my non-Muslim grandmother in India, which itself is testament to the wideness of his appeal. She would never have offered *Muhammad*—Muhammad was for believers. *Ali* was for all. On that first morning, watching Khuder kiss the door of the shrine of Imam Ali, it occurred to me that another way to think of the Sunni-Shiite split was in terms of what had been a recurring theme on this pilgrimage of mine—namely, the ancient division between materiality and pure abstraction that had riven Byzantine Christianity no less than Islam. On the one hand were shrines, images, sacred objects; on the other, a fierce love of formlessness born out of a loathing of consecrated ground, idols, and clergy. The Wahhabis, who dominate the religious landscape of Saudi Arabia, practice an extreme form of Sunni Islam. To them, even the Prophet's house in Medina could be destroyed without a thought (as it was in 1925) lest it become a shrine. Shiite Islam, by contrast, is a religion of touch and physicality, of clergy and sacra. People here made *turbah*s (clay tablets) from the earth of the two shrine cities of Najaf and Karbala. In this culture of the physical imbued with the sacred, Najaf and Karbala, with their grand ayatollahs and seminaries, along with the mosque in Kufa, where Ali died, form the points of a sacred triangle.

Later that morning, we left Najaf through its vast necropolis, roughly four square miles of graveyard, with earth-rimmed roads running like avenues past graves of varying shapes and sizes, some simple constructions of brick and marble, others as big as mausoleums. Driving down the forty-five-mile road to Karbala, every inch of it lined with resting places for pilgrims, some mere sheds, some grand structures, I was confronted by another unintended symmetry of this pilgrimage: the return of the sacred, despite great political and historical upheaval. Iraq is one of four Shiite-majority nations in the world, the others being Iran, Bahrain, and Azerbaijan. Saddam Hussein had deprived the Shiites of what was something of a holy land to them. When he fell, there had been a spontaneous eruption of Shiite pilgrimage. This year, the Arbaeen would welcome as many as 25 million people, making it the largest annual pilgrimage in the world. When I expressed my wonder that such a vast event could have been suppressed, Khuder said, "It happened, but in secret." He himself had done it on multiple occasions, picking his way through fields at night.

I had so far avoided the subject of the US occupation of Iraq but, on the road to Karbala, Khuder began pointing to places where he had seen special operations involving Apache helicopters, or where, in the center of Najaf in 2004, he had witnessed a brutal showdown between the Mahdi Army, led by the cleric Muqtada al-Sadr, and US forces with Abrams tanks. We had a young, restless driver whom Khuder kept chiding for his inability to sit still. That, he remembered, was what had gotten a driver he used to work with killed at a US checkpoint. Upon hearing this, our driver, who loved biker stunts and made TikTok videos, casually said that his father had been killed by Abu Musab al-Zarqawi, the Jordanian founder of al-Qaeda in Mesopotamia whose hatred of Shiites was legendary. "Madness," Khuder said, "tragedy in every house." The Shiite pilgrimages of Ashura and Arbaeen had themselves been targeted several times since 2003 by al-Qaeda and ISIS—and with each attack the Shiites, whose faith had been born in tragedy, drew an inexorable line to the primal sacrifice of Hussein.

Outside the gilded dome and red air-conditioned maw of the shrine of Imam Hussein in Karbala, William was stopped on account of his camera. "They're worried about tatbir," Khuder said. "They're afraid it will give the wrong impression." The head-cutting practice remains controversial even among Shiites and has been banned in Iran by Ayatollah Ali Khamenei since 1994. Standing in the afternoon sun, I felt a chill as I saw younger and younger boys go by, dressed conspicuously in white, like sacrificial victims, in anticipation of performing tatbir. One boy actor, dressed in a green sequined tunic and a metallic helmet with a white plume, was surrounded by squadrons of drummers and flagellants beating their backs rhythmically with symbolic cat-o'-nine-tails called *zanjeer*s. Another man, with a tank on his back bearing the image of Hussein with flowing hair and beard, threaded a course through the pilgrims, spraying them with rose water. Some mawkibs were handing out ice water, others, with garish signs, the lettering dripping red paint, poured lamentations into the street through loudspeakers: "We love you, Imam Hussein, with our body, our spirit, our blood." As Khuder wrangled with the authorities, trying to persuade them to let William bring his camera into the shrine, I felt I understood the role of blood in the Shiite scheme. It was the ultimate line of continuity, a vessel for the transmission of memory, as well as raw genetic material—it spoke to that question of lineage that had torn apart the early Muslim world.

When finally we were let through, we found ourselves on a palm-lined concourse. A red carpet, with misters overhead, led between the shrines of Hussein and his half brother, Abbas. The two-way traffic of pilgrims revealed Omanis in fine-hemmed robes with embroidered caps gliding past ruddy-faced farmers from Multan, Pakistan, stylishly turned out in black and gold. "Look at their faces," Khuder said, overcome by their devotion. "They're poor, but they come thousands of kilometers for the love of Imam Hussein."

PILGRIMAGE WAS A great equalizer. Within the elliptical sphere created by the road in and out of the shrine, a kind of democracy did seem to prevail. Men and women came as one before their maker. Occasionally the spell of equality was broken by the obvious prosperity of Gulf Arabs (or in Bolivia, of the richer Aymara women) in comparison with the poverty of their coreligionists, but it would be churlish not to admit the fellow feeling that pilgrimage engendered. At times, when it was edged with religious passion, it unnerved me. When my father's killer was executed, after many years of delay, there were tens of thousands at his funeral. They used the same title for him that was used here for Hussein—shahid—and there is a shrine in his name on the outskirts of Islamabad where devotees bring offerings. As a result, no doubt, I was suspicious of the kinds of fraternities that religion fosters. In Karbala, I certainly felt a sense of shared humanity, but I never doubted it was an illusion. Even within Islam, on that concourse between the two shrines, the promise of fraternity was belied by the tales I heard of the oppression that Shiites faced at the hands of Sunni majorities.

Twenty-three-year-old Farman Ahsan, with a prominent black mustache, had come by car from Lahore (my father's hometown) via Iran, stopping along the course of a monthlong journey to do *ziyarat*, visiting Shiite holy places. "In Pakistan, you know how it is?" he said to me. "They throw stones at us. We need a permit to do anything. Here we're free, we can do *maatam* [mourning rituals] wherever we want." There was the nineteen-year-old Muhammad, who had come the long way to Iraq from Saudi Arabia via Kuwait using removable paper visas to avoid detection in his own country. "Otherwise, they kill him," Khuder said, laughing mirthlessly. In Karbala, I

met Syed Salman Raza—a Pakistani Shiite from Karachi—
who had been coming to the shrine city for thirty-five years.
He had seen it littered with bodies in 1991, when Saddam,
in the wake of his invasion of Kuwait, brutally crushed the
Shiite uprising, killing as many as 150,000. In his fifties now,
he remembered having to bribe Saddam's spies in order to perform the basic rites of Ashura. "We had to pay them just to
be allowed to wear black," he said, "and we were forbidden
from talking to any Iraqis." Raza also spoke of "the revolution
of Imam Hussein." When I asked him what made it revolutionary, he said, "It gives every oppressed man the courage to
stand up to his oppressor."

As Ashura approached, the warlike atmosphere in Najaf
reached a fever pitch. Empty days of blinding-white heat gave
way to nights of blood and ferment. The number of knife
sharpeners in the side streets multiplied, even as the age of
those with shaved patches on their heads, wearing what I now
recognized as the white vestments of tatbir, fell into the single
digits. "Why are they so young?" I asked Khuder.

"They want them to not forget Imam Hussein," he said.

A field hospital had materialized opposite the entrance
to the holy shrine, ready for the bloodletting that was to ensue. Everywhere I could hear swords being drawn from their
scabbards and the swooshing and hissing of blades slicing the
torrid night air. Every evening outside of the shrine, we had
seen two or three flagellants, some seeming almost to dance as
they flicked flails equipped with blades across their backs. As
the night of Ashura descended upon us, the scale of what was
about to happen became clear. I had my heart in my mouth

as I watched boys of twelve and younger approach a bald mustachioed man sitting at a stall like a street barber and wince as he used a dagger to draw blood lines across the patches of shaved head they proffered him.

Then, at sunset, it began. Men came in battalions, some carrying gilded replicas of holy shrines, some led by the haunting figure of Imam Hussein in a white veil holding the arrow-pierced body of his infant in his hands. Behind him were streets full of men and boys in white bleeding from their heads. They seemed just to tap their scalps with their daggers, even as they dug deeper into preexisting wounds.

William and I wandered through neighborhood gatherings, where children with batons danced around a strongman bearing a mashael that dripped fire and oil. We saw grown men faint and be carried out by other bleeding men, their chests hard with the rust of dried blood. The security was heavy. Iraq's interior minister was in town from Baghdad for the big night. We passed clothes racks hung with robes for those ready to exchange their funereal black for sacrificial white.

Around 1:00 a.m., Khuder dropped us off at our hotel, imploring us not to step outside until he returned in the morning. A Russian Israeli doctoral student at Princeton had been kidnapped in Baghdad earlier this year, and throughout our time in Iraq, Khuder told anyone who asked that I was "Pakistani" and William "Cambodian." "We have to be careful," he said cryptically when I asked why, but I sensed it was his way of dissociating us from rich countries that could pay large ransoms.

From the tinted windows of the hotel lobby we watched a predawn procession of men, hundreds upon hundreds, in states of elation and rapture, laughing, weeping, bleeding. The day broke over a ghost town whose dusty streets were full of oil stains and blood-soaked rags. Khuder picked us up just before 9:00 a.m. to take us to a passion play, known as a *tash-abih*. Now and then, we passed an impeccably dressed cleric in light, floating robes with a black turban and green scarf. In his wake, like survivors of a carnage, came bandaged, blood-ied men, their arms draped over one another, making their way home as if from a night of revelry.

At the edge of town, an air-conditioned walkway, akin to what one might find at the airport in Doha, Qatar, led to a desolate stretch of pale, hummocked land enclosed by barbed wire. Beyond was the Sea of Najaf, a brackish lake, glittering feverishly in the distance. On a natural stage of sorts, fash-ioned from ravined earthen walls, a captivated audience in black of some several hundred formed a perimeter, while fa-miliar short plays unfolded below them. The forces of Yazid, in yellow and red, as if color itself were a sign of corruption, were arrayed against Hussein's beleaguered camp with satin flags in green, black, and white. With every death, the women of the house, in white gloves and veils, ran between the battle-field and the tents emitting wails of sorrow into a loudspeaker. The role of Zaynab, Hussein's sister and the Prophet's grand-daughter, was especially important. It was she who would live to tell the tale—she who would protect Hussein's sole surviv-ing son, Ali Zayn al-Abidin, who was too sick to fight, and thereby the bloodline of the Prophet. With each loss of life, Hussein addressed the audience, who stood agog in the heat with cardboard boxes over their heads to shield them from the fierce morning sun, asking if anyone was with him or whether he was alone. "Labaik, ya Hussein," came the solemn chorus of surrounding voices. It was a theater of the people in that most affecting sense, where even the poverty of the staging—the sun-bleached flags, the crackling loudspeaker, the melodrama, and the audience in thrall—served only to deepen the pathos. On our return through the now-deserted town, we saw the field hospital had been cleared away.

I was never more aware than at that moment of the creative power of pilgrimage. We think of tradition as static, its rituals fixed for the ages, but in fact within certain parameters it is constantly evolving, incorporating new elements and technologies. It was this inner vitality—"the modernity of tradition," to borrow a phrase from the American political scientists Lloyd and Susanne Rudolph—that gives pilgrimage its ability to endure. Whether through the introduction of vodka into Mongolian Buddhist ritual, the use of cellphones and social media to enhance the performative aspects of Ashura, or even the spirit of one pilgrimage resurrected in another, as in the case of fiesta in Copacabana, the survival of pilgrimage depended on its talent for balancing continuity with change.

The last night—Zaynab's night—belonged to women. "Never was there a woman of Zaynab's courage," Zahraa, a twenty-two-year-old accounting student who co-owns a flower and gift shop in Najaf, said to me on the night of Ashura. "She's an inspiration to all women." We sat in Cafe Maram, a modern coffee shop hung with fake pink blossoms. Zahraa, whose family had a mawkib on the road to Karbala, was dressed in a black abaya. Khuder had discouraged me from approaching women during my time in Iraq—"It's not in the culture"—but Zahraa seemed keen to talk. When I asked her how Ashura was for women, she said it was a quieter affair that played out in houses, with older women taking the role of the sheikh, and of the attendees together reading the "Ziyarat-e-Hussein," an homage in verse to Hussein. Did she want to join the mayhem outside, I asked.

"No," she scoffed, her face brimming with amusement, adding flatly, in relation to tatbir, "It's wrong."

Khuder, who was translating, nodded. "I agree."

A new flag—red letters against a white ground that read HAIDAR, a name for Ali, which, Khuder explained, was what people said when they practiced tatbir—rose over Karbala. After the male hysteria of the hours before, there was a feeling of exhalation. "We feel Imam Mahdi is here, even though we can't see him," an Omani pilgrim said to me, referring to the twelfth and last imam, whom the majority of Shiites believe was occulted in the tenth century and who would return at the day of judgment astride a white horse. In that lighter air of expiation, women lit candles on the edge of the street that led from the shrine to the place that marked Hussein's camp on the field of battle. Vendors sold balloons bearing Hussein's likeness. Drifting past us in their abayas, a few women stopped to rock a cradle that contained a plastic doll wrapped in green gauze, standing in for Hussein's slain baby.

I WAS IN the final hours of my six-month pilgrimage, and certain historical synchronicities were coalescing. It was here in Iraq in 1258 that Hulegu the Mongol, Genghis Khan's grandson, shattered the power of the Arab Muslim empire by destroying its capital at Baghdad. In accordance with the Mongol prohibition against spilling royal blood, the last caliph with wide acceptance among a majority of Muslims was wrapped in a carpet and trampled to death. Only ten years before, on the far western edge of the Muslim world, Ferdinand III of Castile—the patron saint of what would be called La Reconquista—had, with the exception of Granada, brought five and a half centuries of Islamic rule on the Iberian Peninsula to an end in Seville. It was that revitalized Catholic Spain that went on to conquer the Incas of the Altiplano, sowing the seed of its zealotry in the New World. These were the accidents of history, the butterfly effect that ran through the three very different societies to which my pilgrimage had taken me. The Shiite movement, which the writer Vali Nasr has described as an ethno-racial protest of a newly subjugated people (Persians, namely) against Arab rule, was a prequel to these intersecting histories—and, as the darker, bloodier hours of Ashura unfolded, I was struck by what William said: "It's a protest. They want to be seen." Ashura is both protest and theater, but that does nothing to diminish its power.

Back in January, I had begun this pilgrimage full of modern fears related to faithlessness and the heightened sense of individuality that prevails in the West. I did not feel like that by the time I left Najaf. I had glimpsed something in Iraq, something I felt as true, inexpressible, and frightening, which I knew would soon be lost to me. It had less to do with faith than with the sheer communal power of the medieval world. If pilgrimage, as anthropologists Victor and Edith Turner write, is meant to be "a release from the ingrown ills of home"—ennui, sameness, predictability—this had certainly been that. It had forced unassimilable dualities upon me: of the sacred and the profane, experience and innocence, wonder and fear, the primeval and the modern, Najaf and New York. It was the discomfort of these irreconcilable realities that gave my pilgrimage its liminal quality. Eduardo Quintela in La Paz had been only half right: pilgrimage did indeed remake my view of reality, but not because a sacred destination had swung into view. It was rather the strain of balancing different planes of existence in my head that put the worries of the past in perspective. The road in and the road out. I now felt an almost sensual longing for the idea of home. Like this night of candles coming after a fever dream, I wanted to be released from the terrifying simultaneity of living between worlds—Bolivia, Mongolia, Iraq—even as I already felt bereft of their intensity.

Watching the desert sun set on my last night in Iraq, color returning magically to the blanched dome of the sky, I thought of my twenty-five-year-old self in Mecca at the beginning of my writing career, assailed by feelings of doubt and inadequacy. Then, I had known the need for a mode of appreciation that lay between dry intellectuality and the ardor of faith, a kind of *felt* thought. We who live in atomized societies, with loneliness and the loss of God, are sometimes prone to fetishizing the passions of societies where rapture lives on. Twenty years later, I could see that it was that same faithlessness, which did not privilege one religion at the cost of another, that had made possible this comparative pilgrimage across three great faiths. It allowed me to see the idea of pilgrimage, in all its richness, as an integral journey, more fundamental to religion than divinity itself.

We tend to think of pilgrimage as a well-trodden path on which only the faithful have the right to travel. In fact, even today, the world is full of people making these intrepid journeys of inner significance, in private and public ways, to see a cherished work of art, to Graceland, to a castle on the coast of Africa where their ancestors were shipped out as slaves to the Americas. If the metaphor of pilgrimage remains as potent as it does today, it is because it speaks to our undiminished need for awe, risk, adventure, and, most of all, a release from the mundanity of our daily lives in order to commune with something sacred. We channel these impulses into modern travel, filling it with expectation and dwelling on its shortcomings. In fact it is we, with our fixed ideas of what travel should give us, who fail the journeys we undertake. The pilgrim spirit is one that wanders away from the comfort and safety of home secure in the knowledge that the transformation the pilgrim will undergo over the course of his journey is the destination. The shrine is a mere decoy. Pilgrimage is above all an inward journey, free of external ideas of outcome: To be disappointed in one's aims only reinforces faith. This is what separates a pilgrimage from a business trip, say. The true lesson of pilgrimage in a secular context instructs us to set out into the world with a questing spirit that is unafraid of looking without finding, allowing curiosity, sympathy, and self-improvement to do the work of faith.

The bravest pilgrims are those who go first, tracing paths

of devotion through a trackless wilderness, inscribing the land with meaning. In those last hours in Iraq, I recalled reading that there had been pilgrims at the site of the Battle of Karbala as early as four years after the massacre, wandering among ghosts, wretched with guilt and grief.

ACKNOWLEDGMENTS

THIS BOOK WOULD NOT HAVE BEEN POSSIBLE WITHOUT the ambition, inspiration and, at times, sheer relentlessness of Hanya Yanagihara. Who else would commission an eighteen-thousand-word piece on pilgrimage? I wish I could say that I had thought of doing the journeys I have done here, but it was Hanya at every step, finding new ways for me to express my concerns as a writer. If these essays are linked by a sub-stratum of connective tissue, related to belonging and syncretism, it is thanks to her. I am also indebted to Thessaly La Force, Jared Hohlt and Deborah Dunn for helping shape and cut the Himalayan drafts I gave them with such sensitivity.

Journeys such as these do not happen without help on the ground. In each place, there were those who set me on my way: Liz Jennings and Asaad Hanna in Turkey; Ahmad Sardar-Afkhami in perfume, Morocco and Mongolia; Alexander

Benaim for perfume; Omar Merouane in Morocco; Reyes Abad and Gioconda Scott in Spain; Basu Ratnam in Mexico; my barber, Farrukh Marupov, in Uzbekistan; Anuk and Amita Arudprgasama and Channa Daswatte in Sri Lanka; Nick Casey in Bolivia; Darshana Narayanan, Nadine Kreisberger and Hamid Sardar-Afkhami in Mongolia; Bobby Ghosh in Iraq.

Finally, I must thank Jacqueline Ko at the Wylie Agency and Kendall Storey at Catapult for seeing the promise of this collection. I was always sure of the inner cohesion of these essays, but it was Jackie and Kendall, and the amazing team at Catapult, who were tasked with the responsibility of convincing the world beyond.

© Ryan Davis

AATISH TASEER is the author of the memoir *Stranger to History*, the acclaimed novels *The Way Things Were*, *The Temple-Goers*, and *Noon*, and the memoir and travelogue *The Twice-Born*. He is a writer at large for *T: The New York Times Style Magazine*. Born in England, raised in New Delhi, and educated in the United States, Taseer now lives in New York.